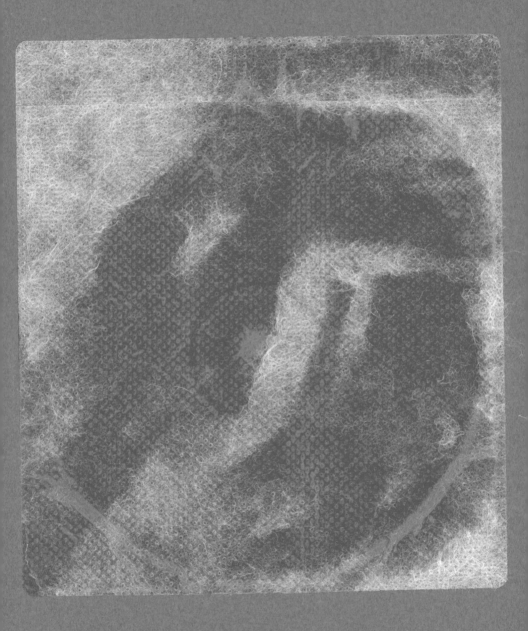

Petit Pattern Book

Petit Pattern Book
Autumn & Winter

Copyright ©2007 2m09cmGRAPHICS, Inc.
www.209g.com

Published in 2007 by BNN, Inc.
1F 35 Sankyo Bldg., 3-7-2, Irifune
Chuo-ku, Tokyo 104-0042 Japan
info@bnn.co.jp
www.bnn.co.jp

Art Direction: Masanari Nakayama (2m09cmGRAPHICS)
Book Design: Makiko Uchida (2m09cmGRAPHICS)
Photo: Sachie Maeda
Pattern Design: 2m09cmGRAPHICS
Edit: Sayaka Ishii
Translation: R.I.C. Publication Asia Co., Inc.

ISBN 978-4-86100-542-8

Printed in Japan by Shinano, Ltd.

おしゃれなパターン素材集

秋・冬

Petit Pattern Book

Autumn & Winter

はじめに

いままでありそうでなかった、おしゃれなパターン素材集。デジタルなの
に、なんだか味のあるパターンたちは、紙に出力するだけで、とってもかわ
いいプリントになります。CD-ROMには、Illustrator用EPSファイルと
Photoshop用JPEGファイルで、本に掲載しているすべてのパターンが
収録されているので、気に入ったパターンをそのまま使うのはもちろん、
色を変えたりサイズを変えたり、自分だけのオリジナルパターンをつくる
こともできます。インテリアのアクセントにしたり、雑貨をリメイクしたり、
大切な人へのプレゼントを包んだり。メインに、背景に、ピンポイントに、
自由なバリエーションで、日々の暮らしにおしゃれなパターンを取り入れて
みてください。

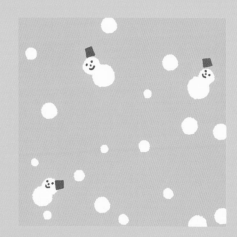

Introduction

A collection of stylish patterns that were once hard to lay hands on is now available to you. Although they are digital images, they all look unique and charming, not at all boring. Just print them out on paper, and you have very cute and attractive prints. You can use the prints to brighten up the inside of your home, revamp your favorite items, or wrap a present for someone special. The prints could be used for creating the main part of a design or background, or as a focal point. Have fun trying out different variations and brighten up your life with these stylish patterns.

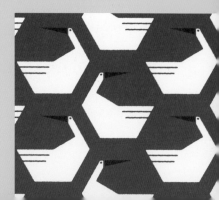

contents

Petit Pattern Book

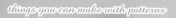

秋
001〜070

Petit Pattern Book
Autumn

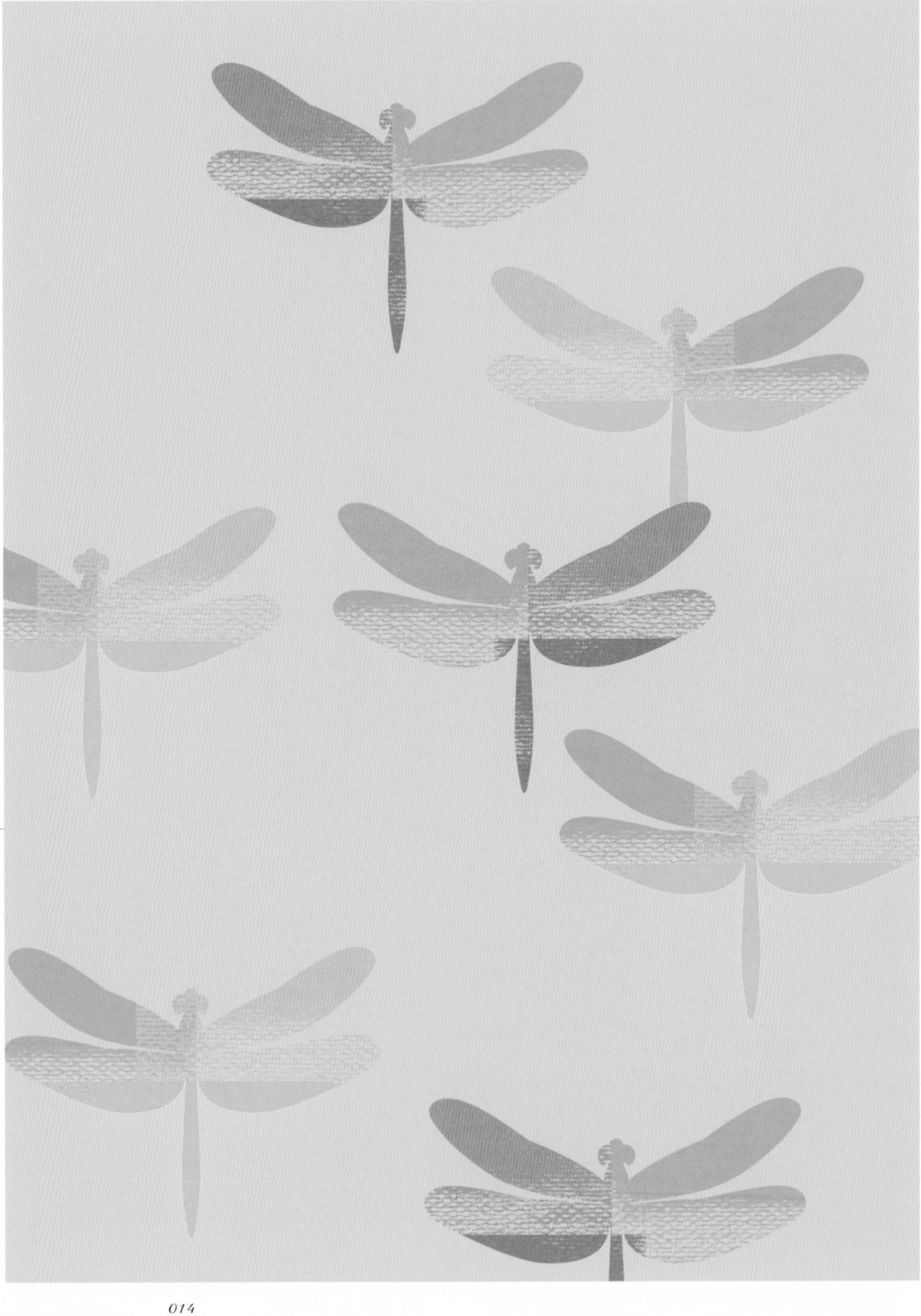

• 001 | 秋 *Autumn*

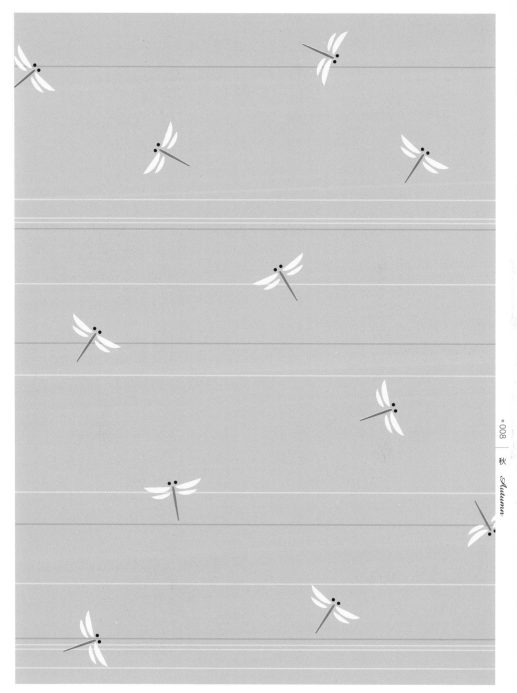

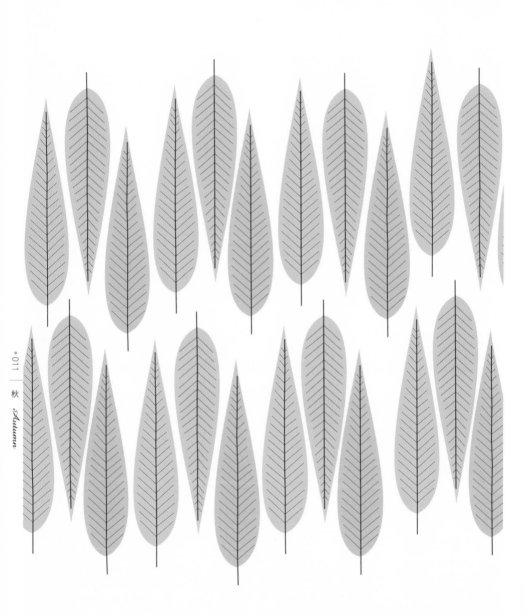

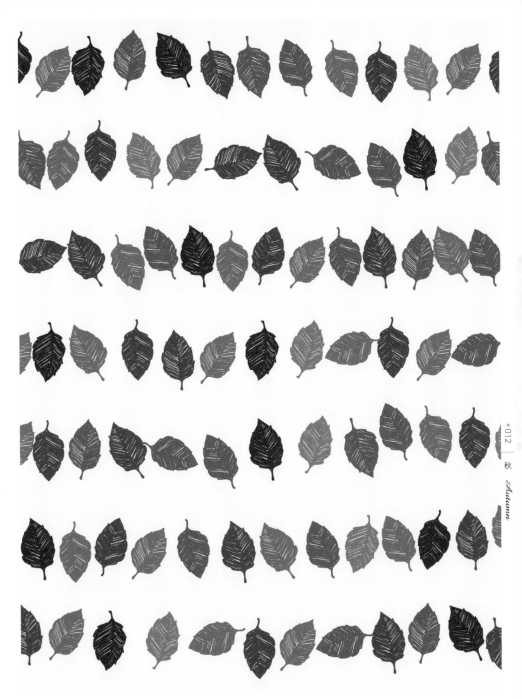

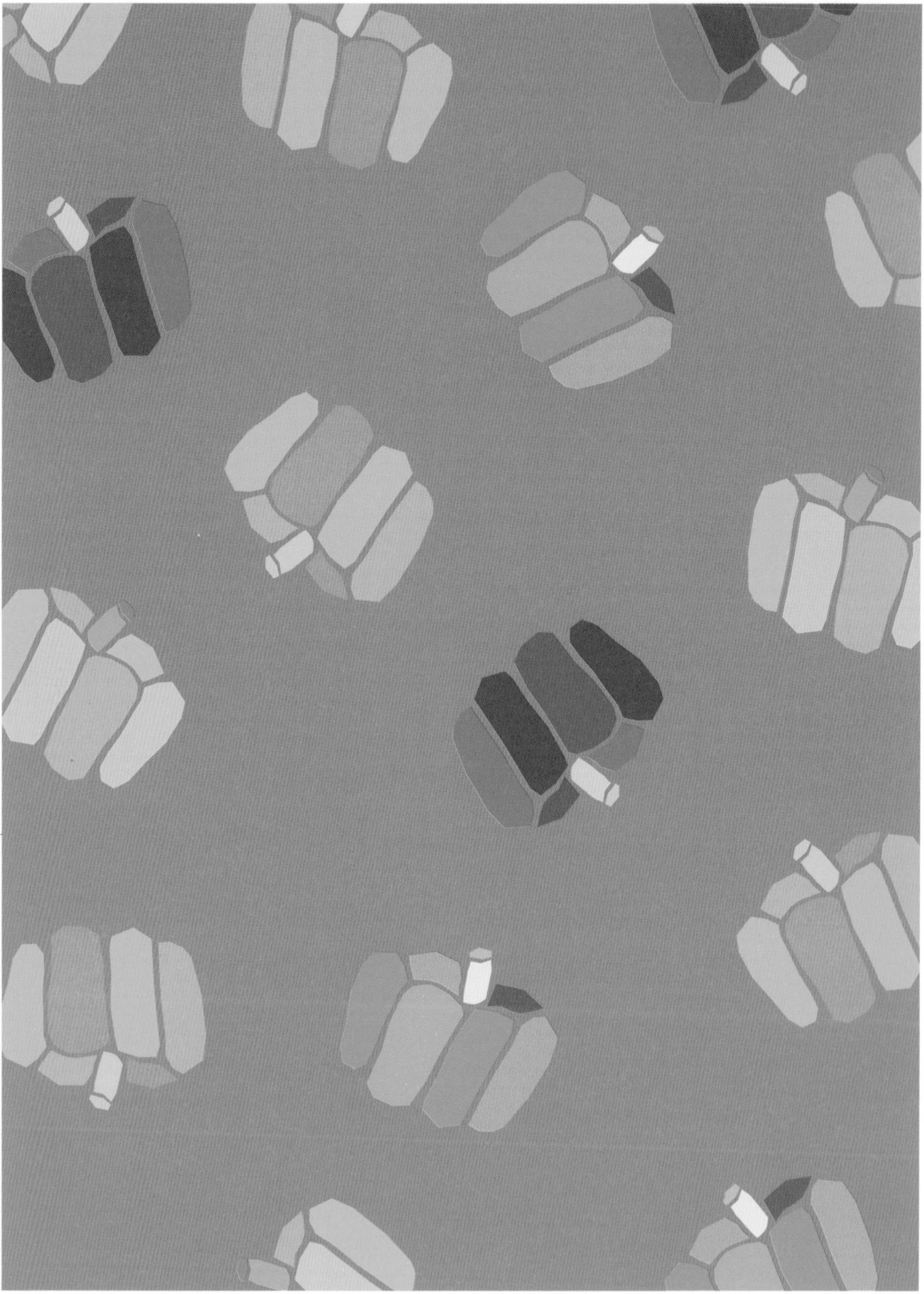

•017 秋 *Autumn*

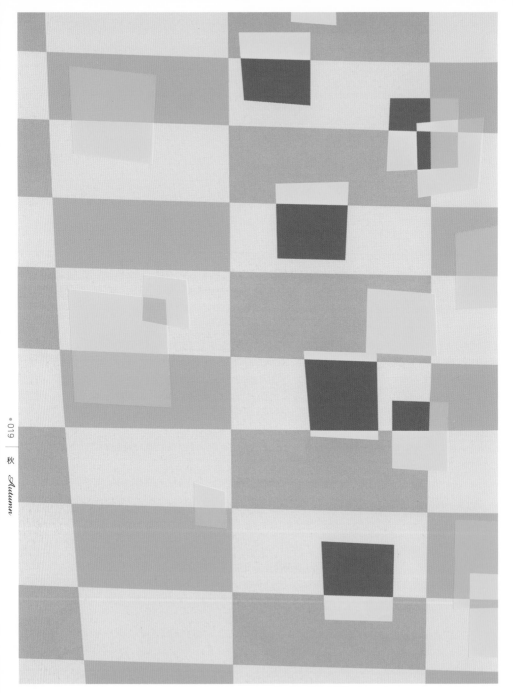

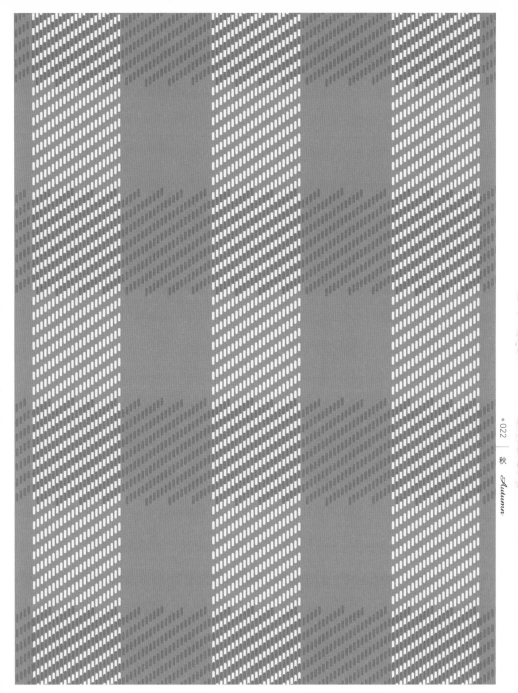

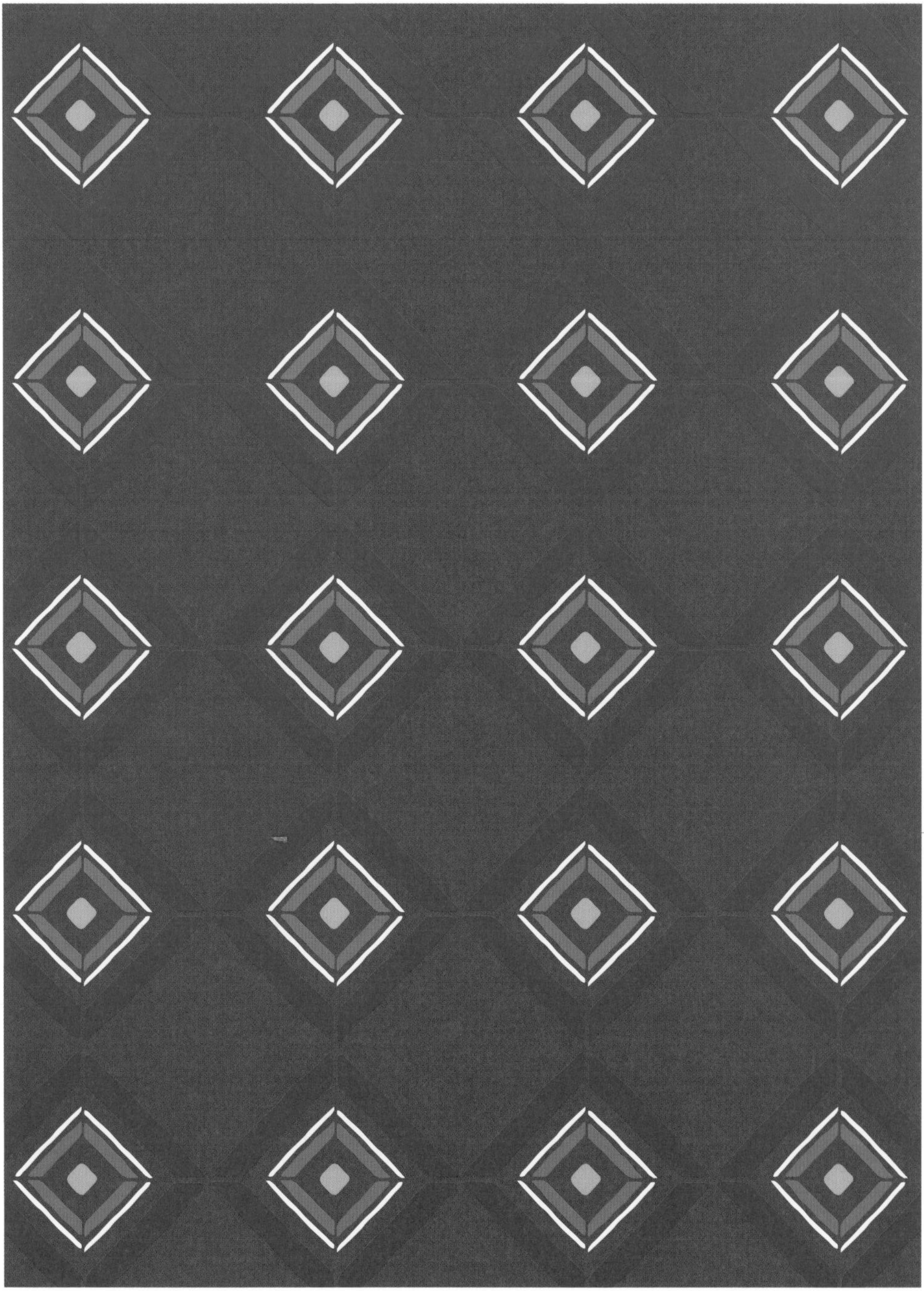

• 024 秋 Autumn

秋
Autumn

秋 *Autumn*

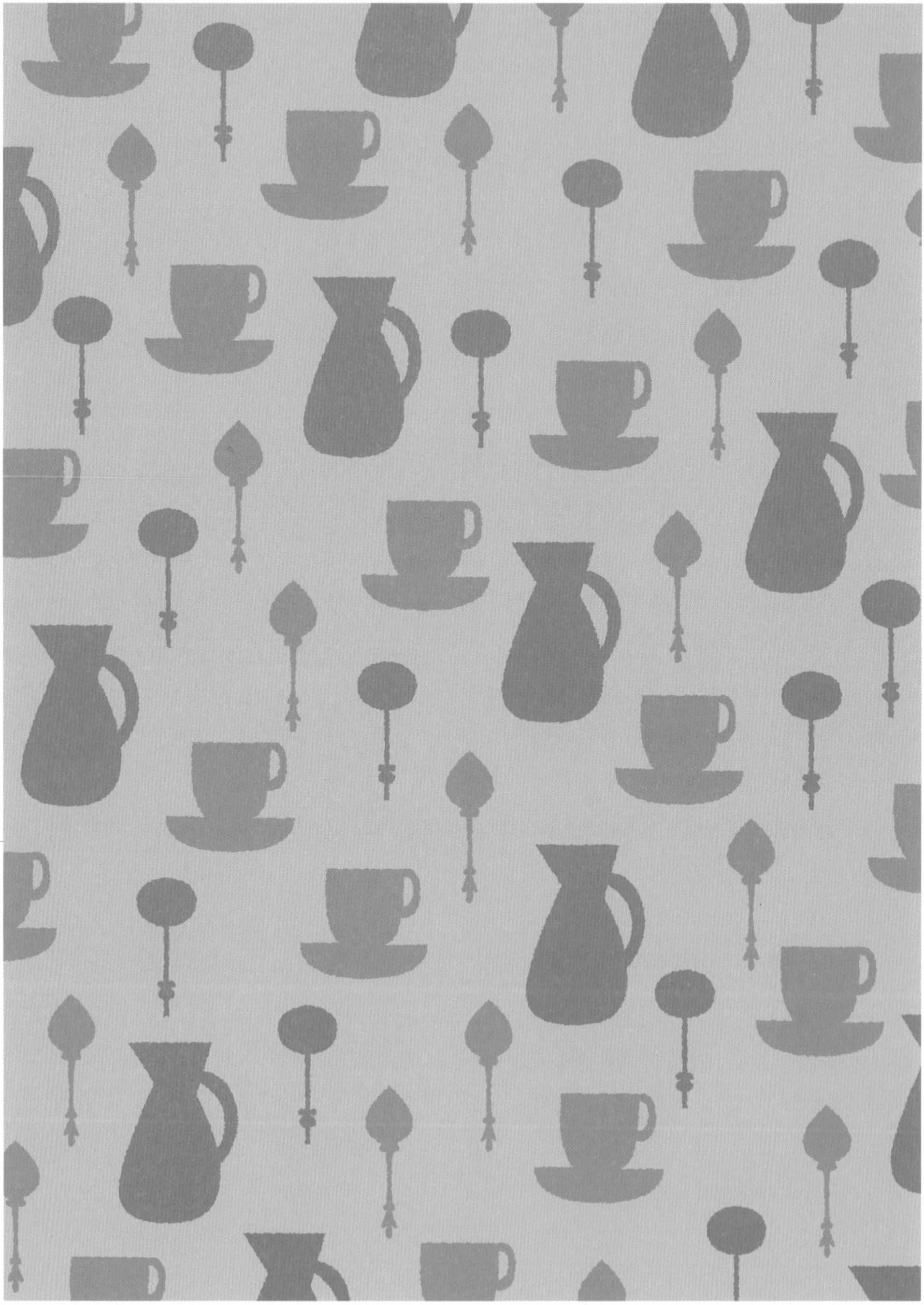

• 033 秋 Autumn

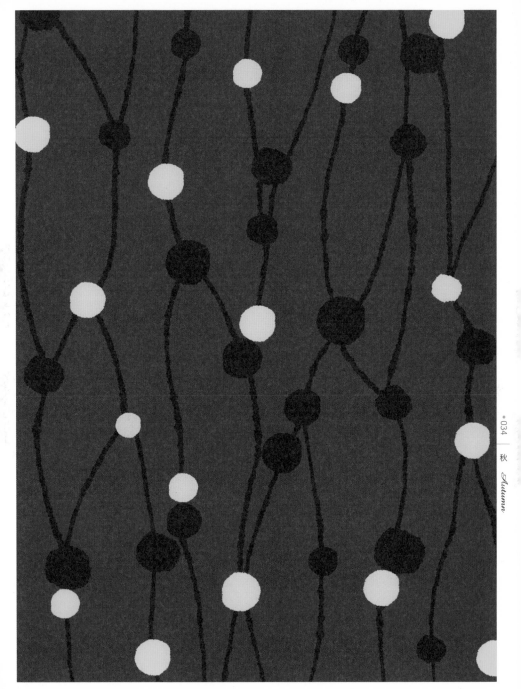

秋 *Autumn*

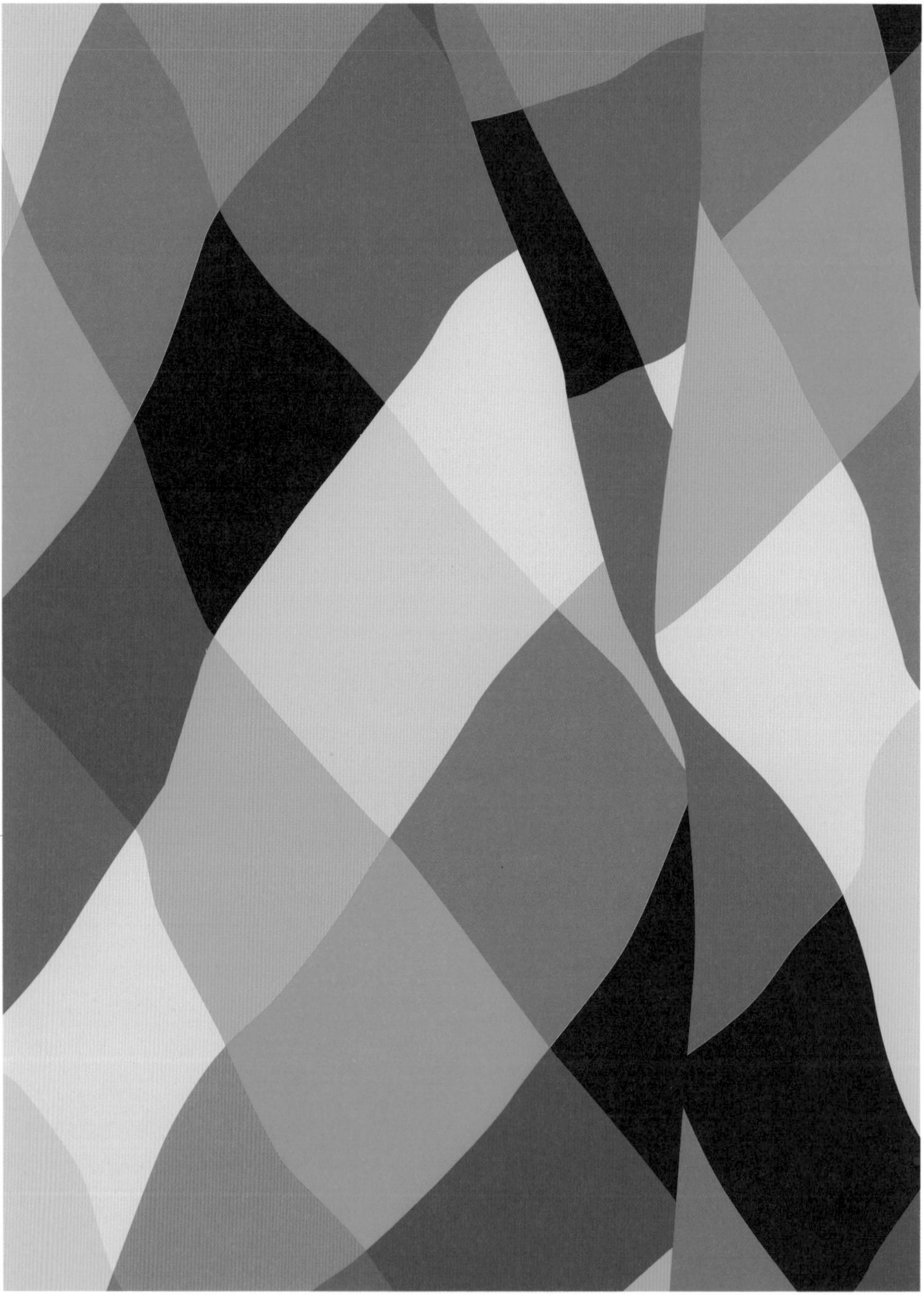

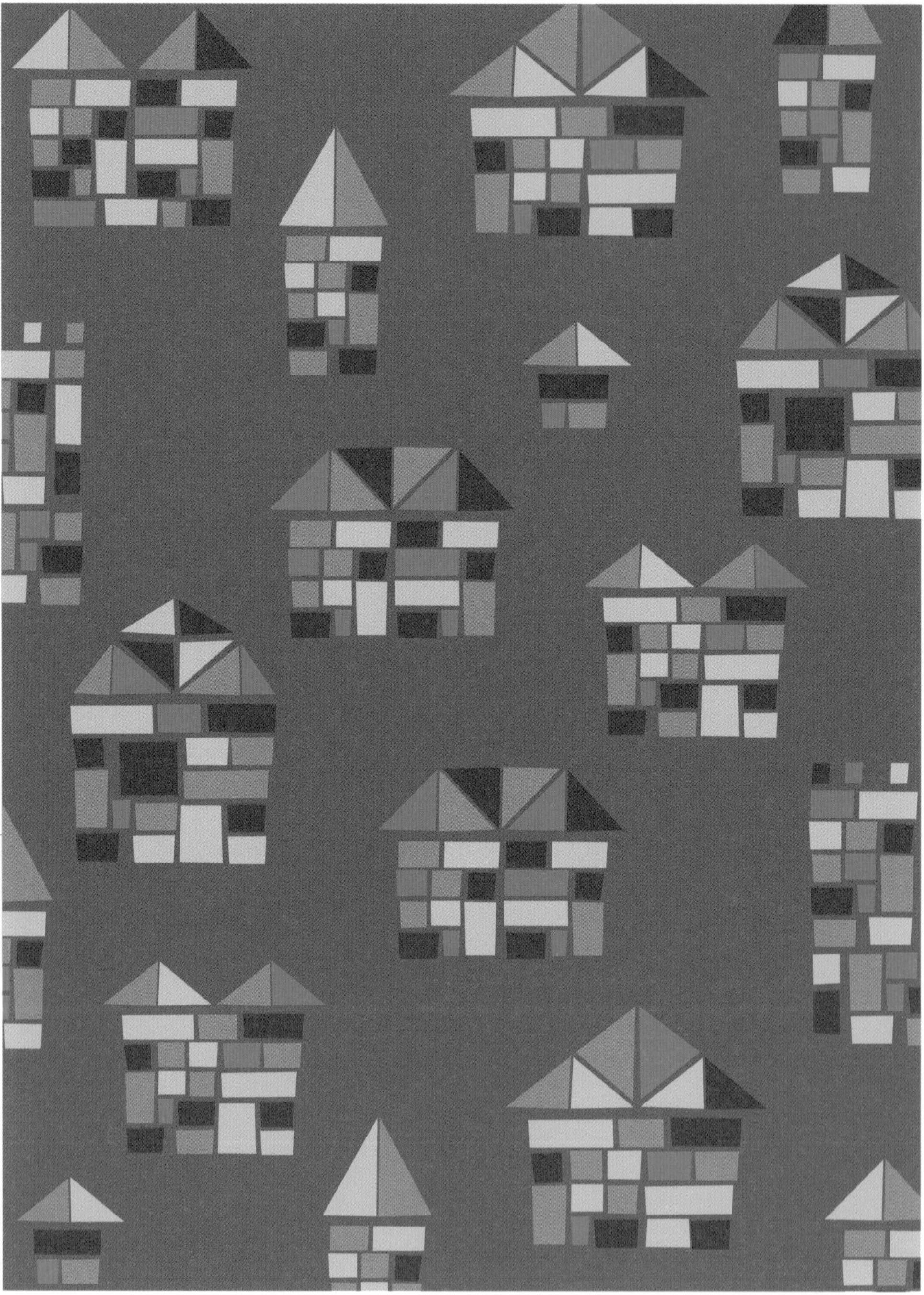

•037 秋 *Autumn*

秋 *Autumn*

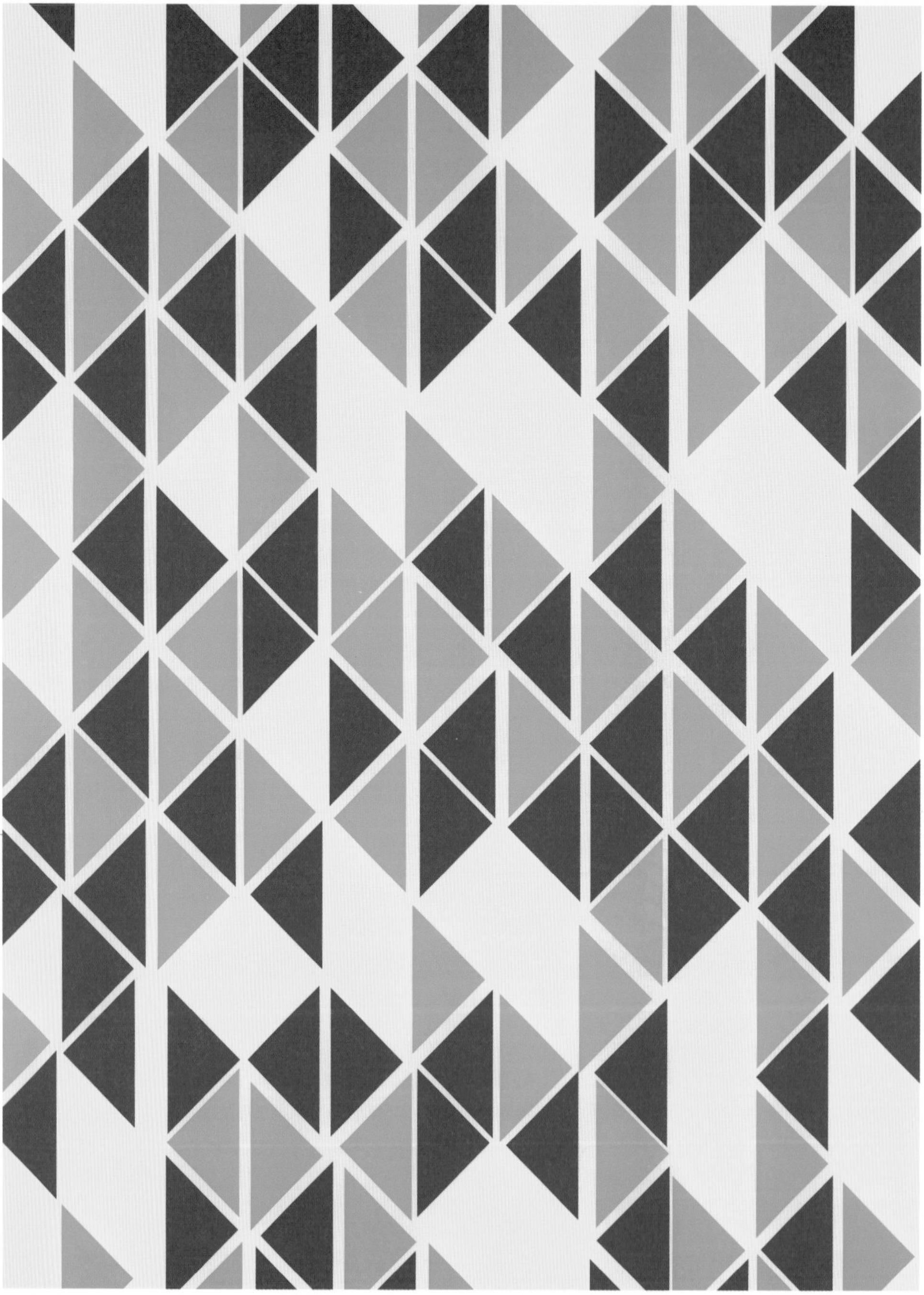

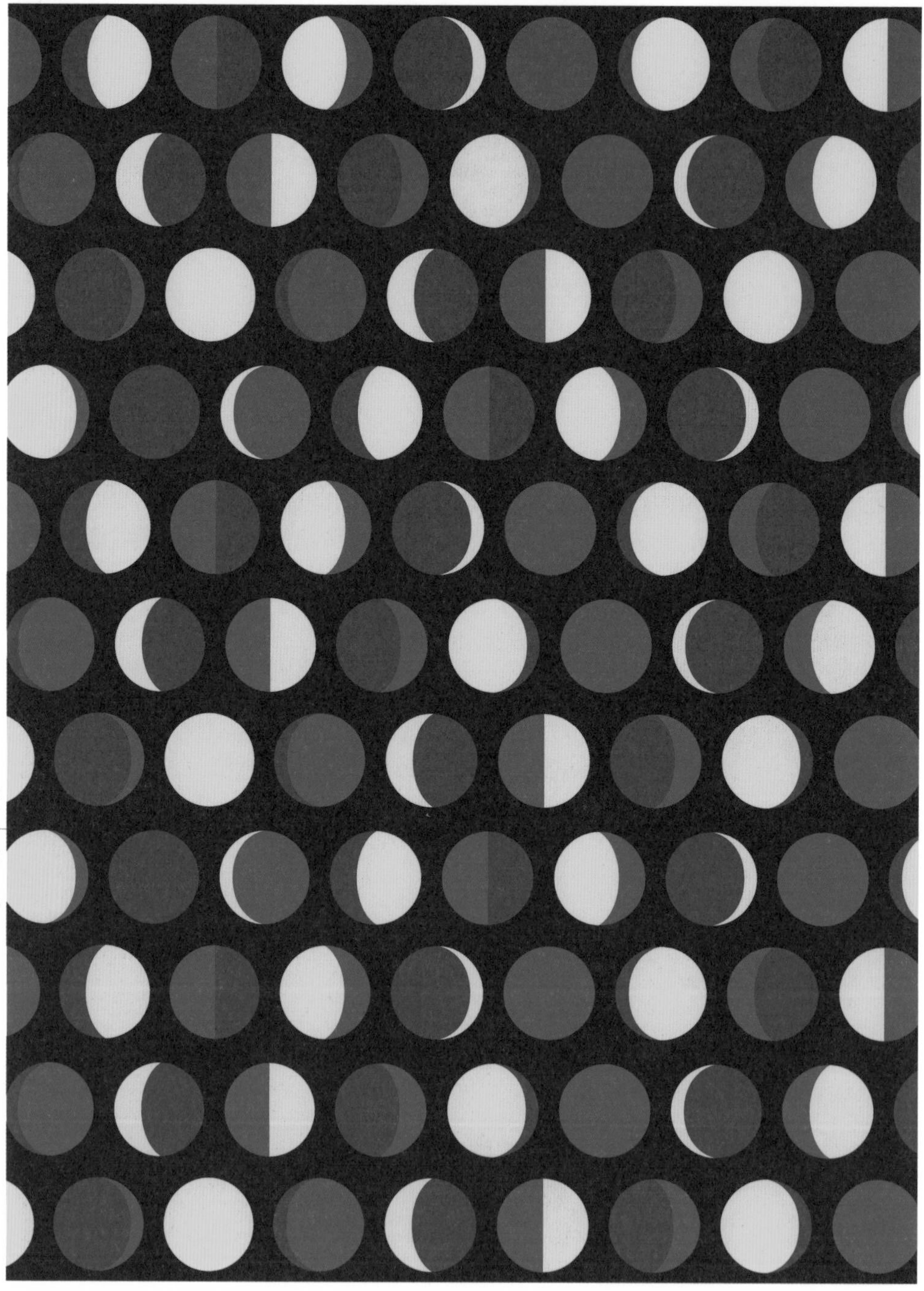

041 秋 *Autumn*

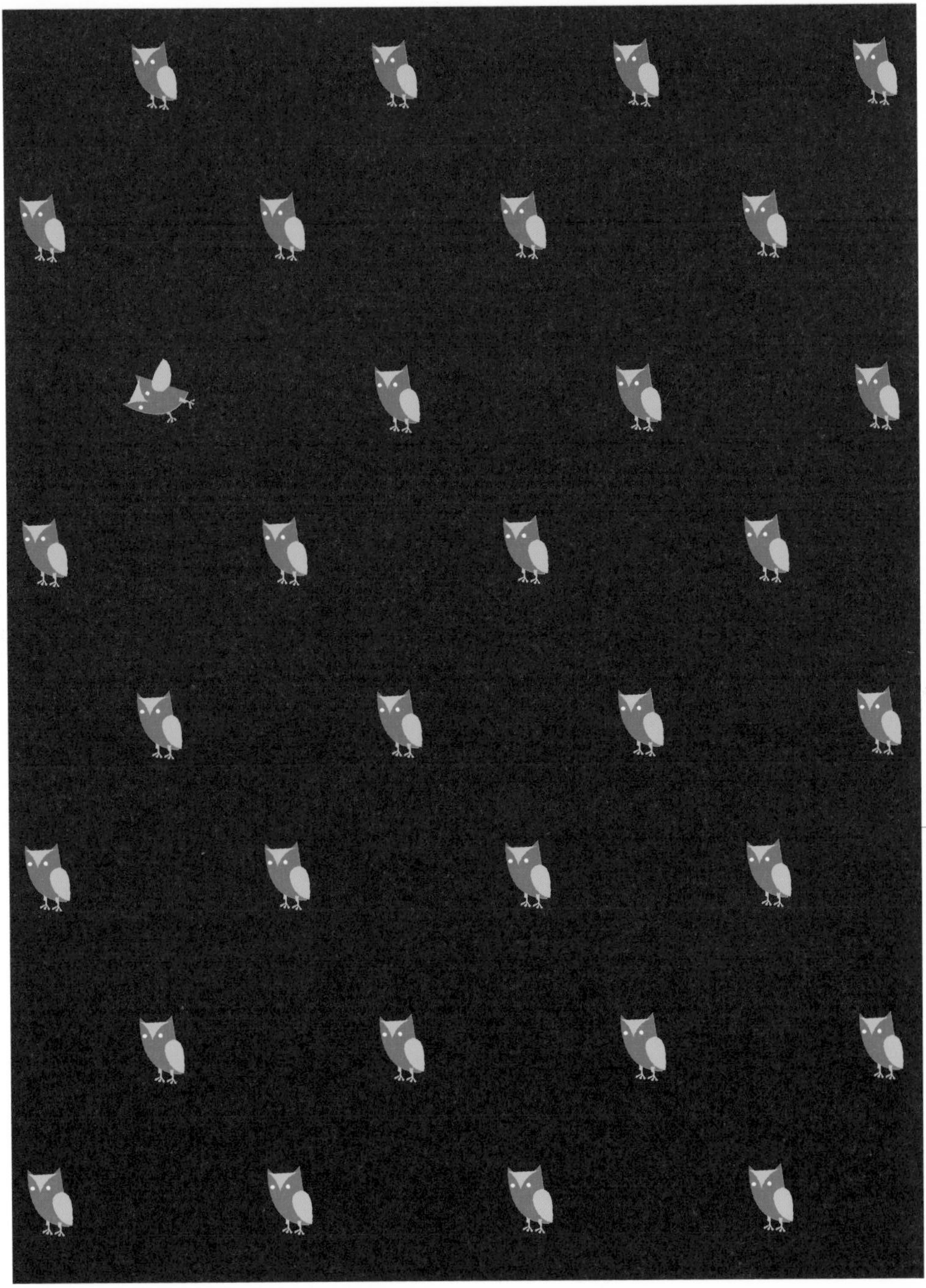

●042 | 秋 *Autumn*

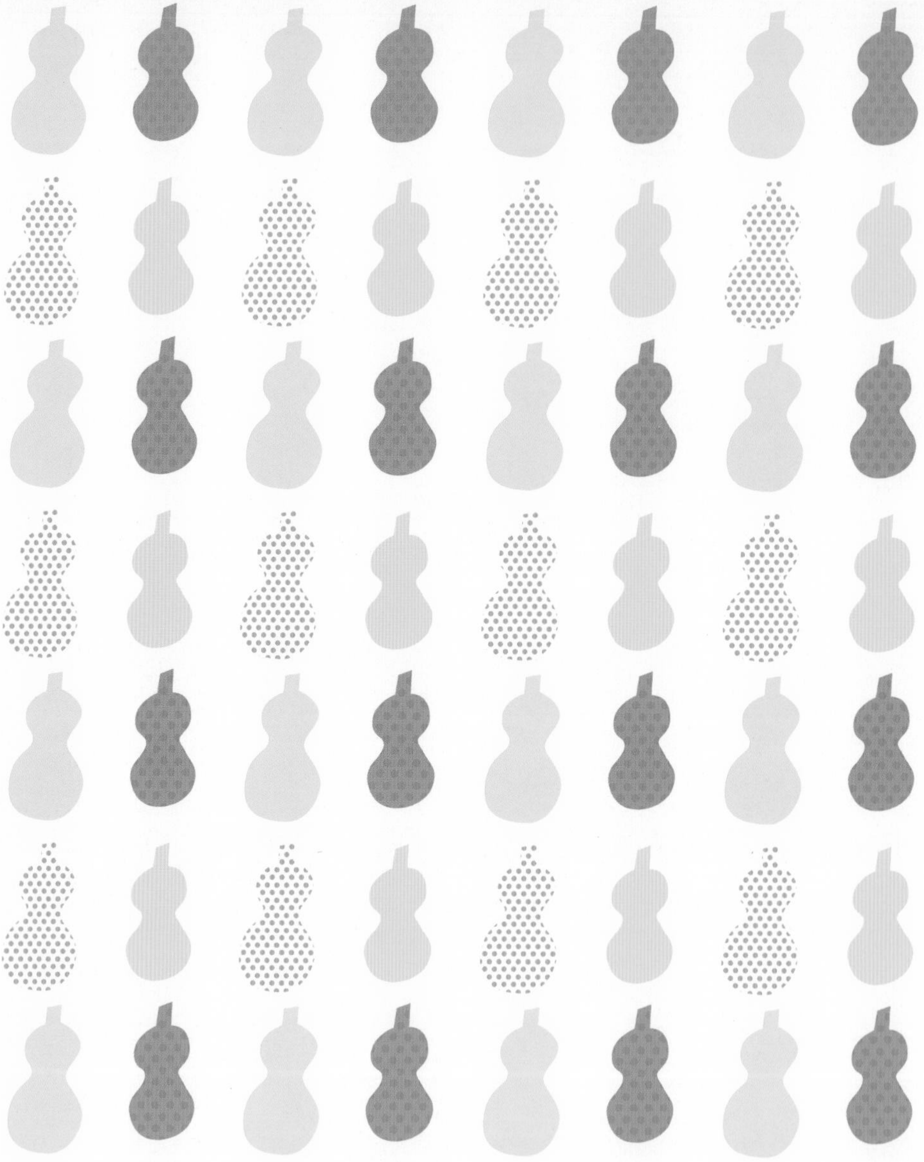

•043 | 秋 *Autumn*

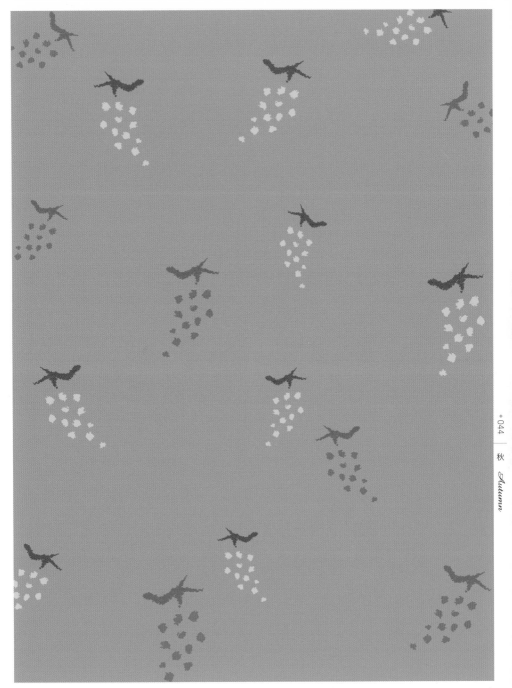

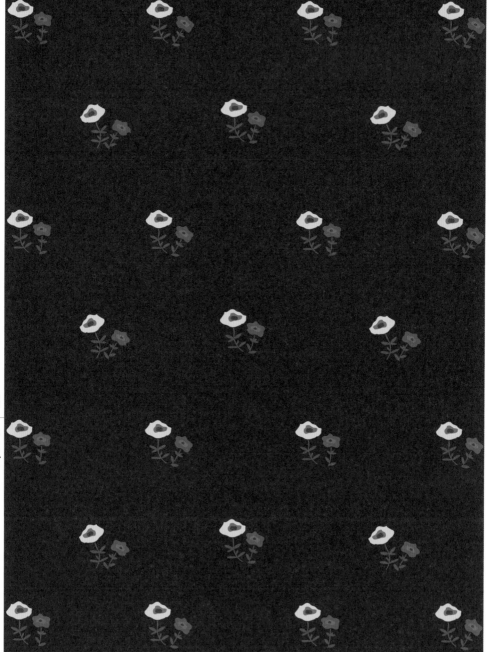

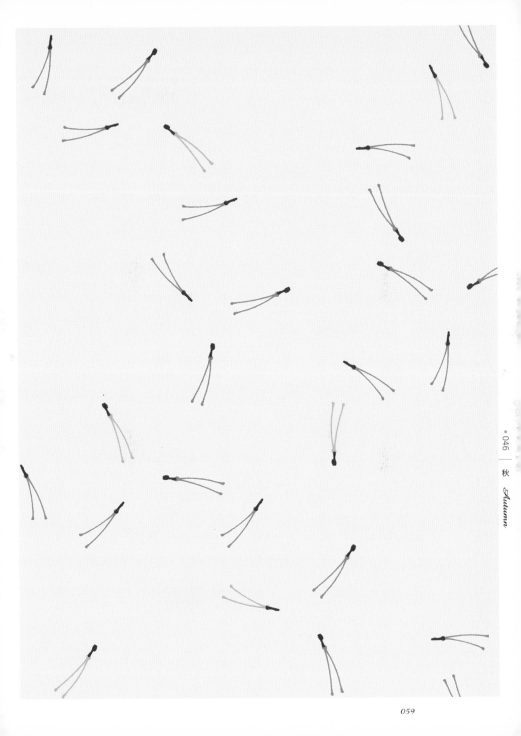

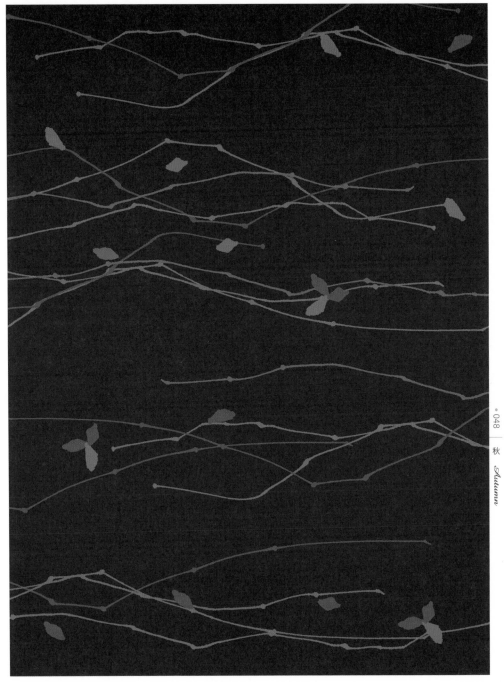

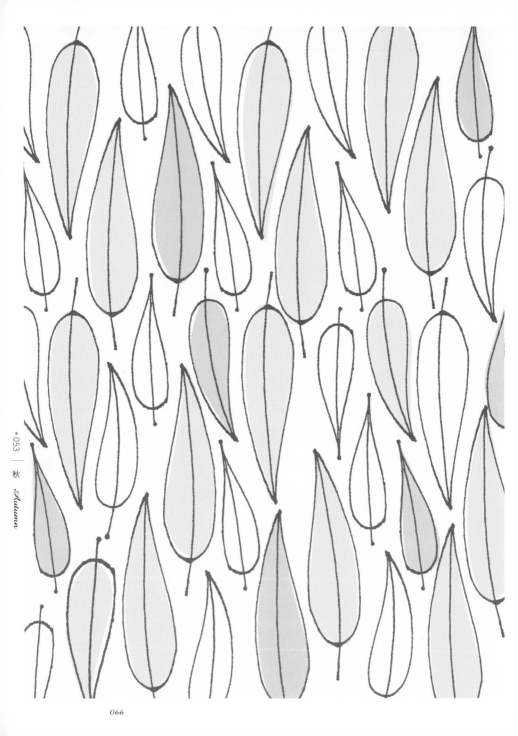

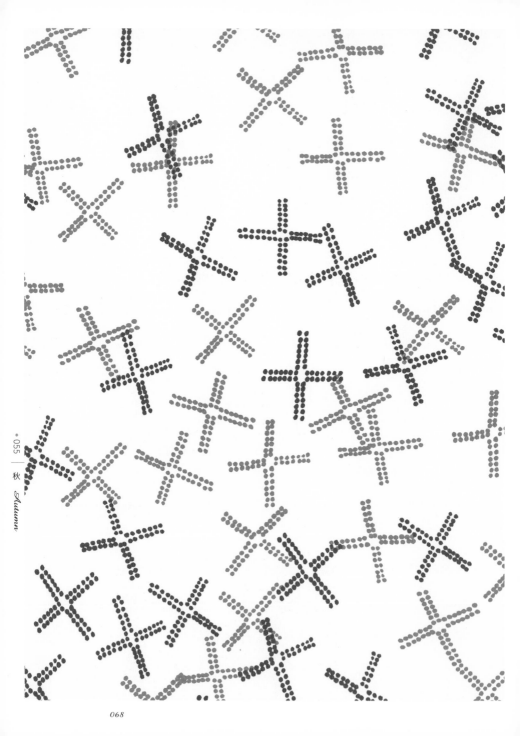

秋 *Autumn*

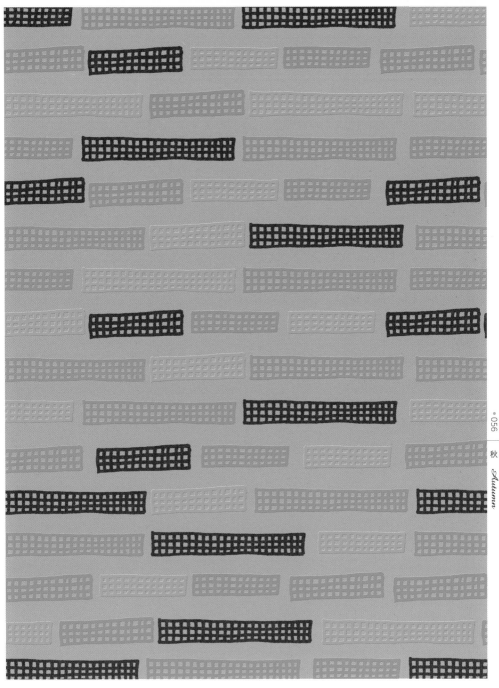

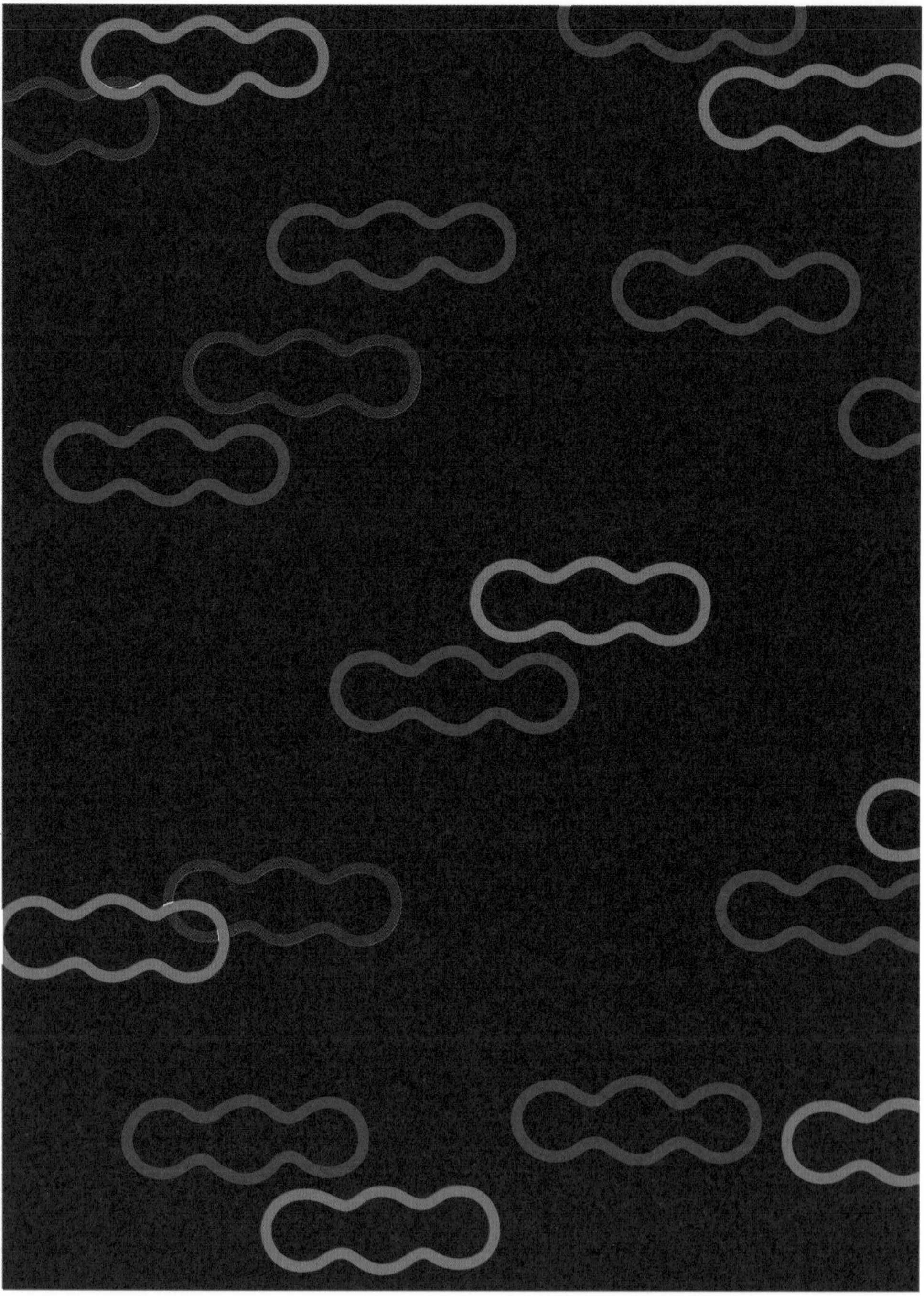

•057 秋 *Autumn*

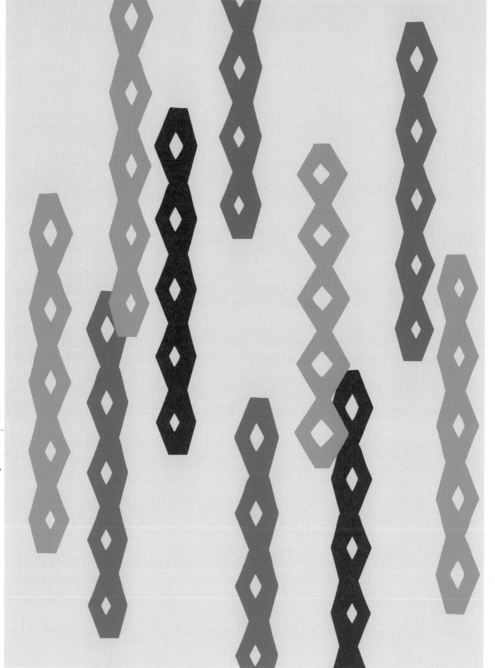

秋 *Autumn*

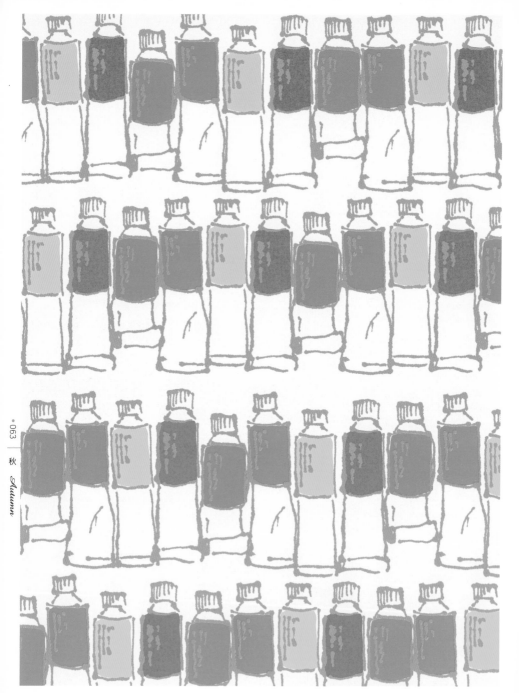

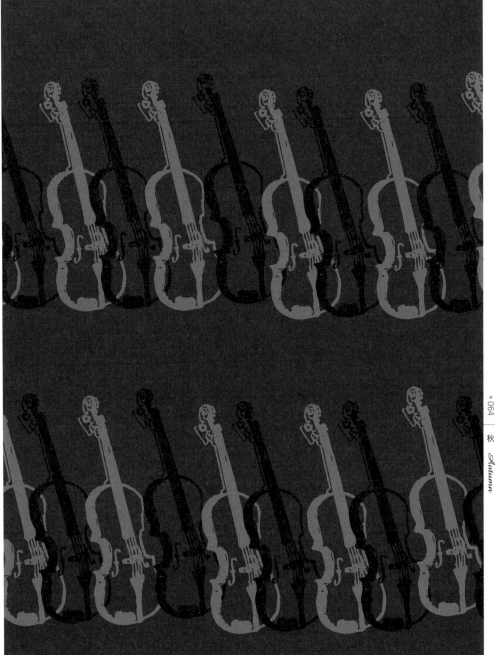

●064

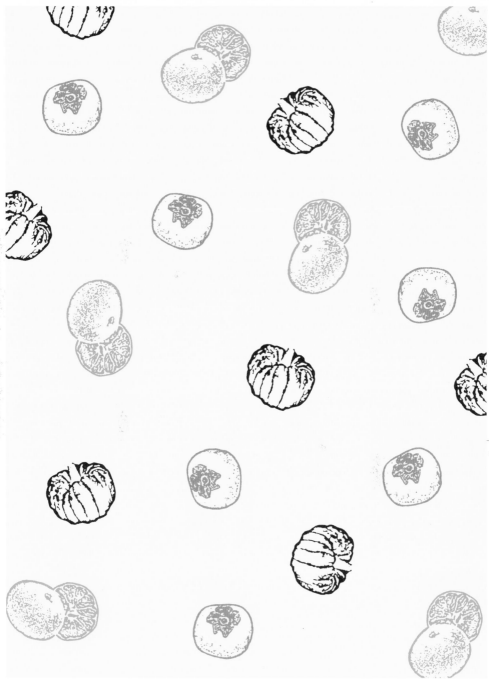

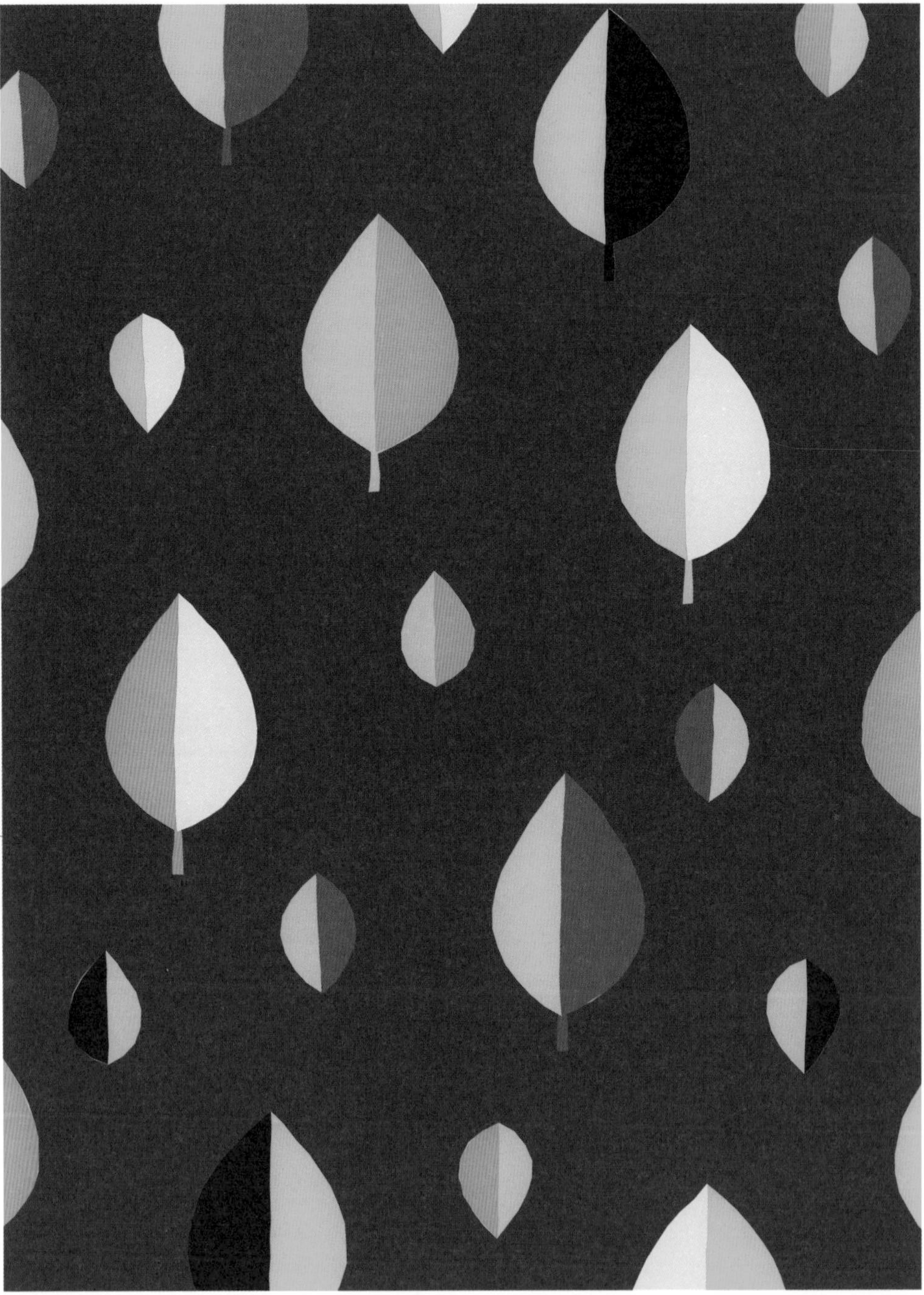

冬
001〜070

Petit Pattern Book
Winter

冬 Winter

• 005 | 冬 Winter

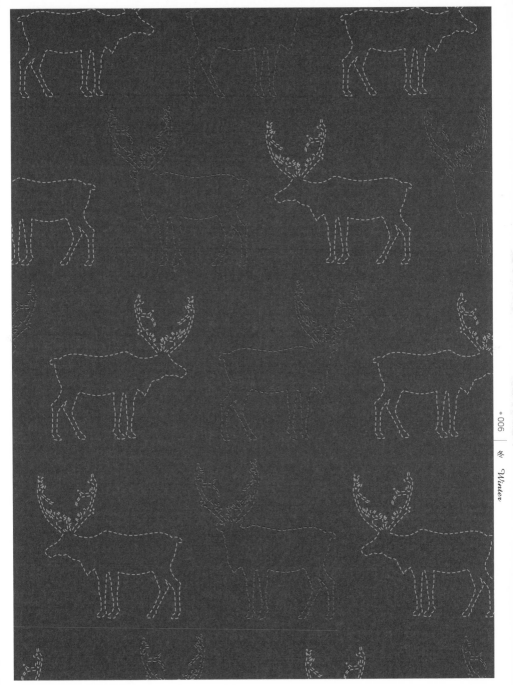

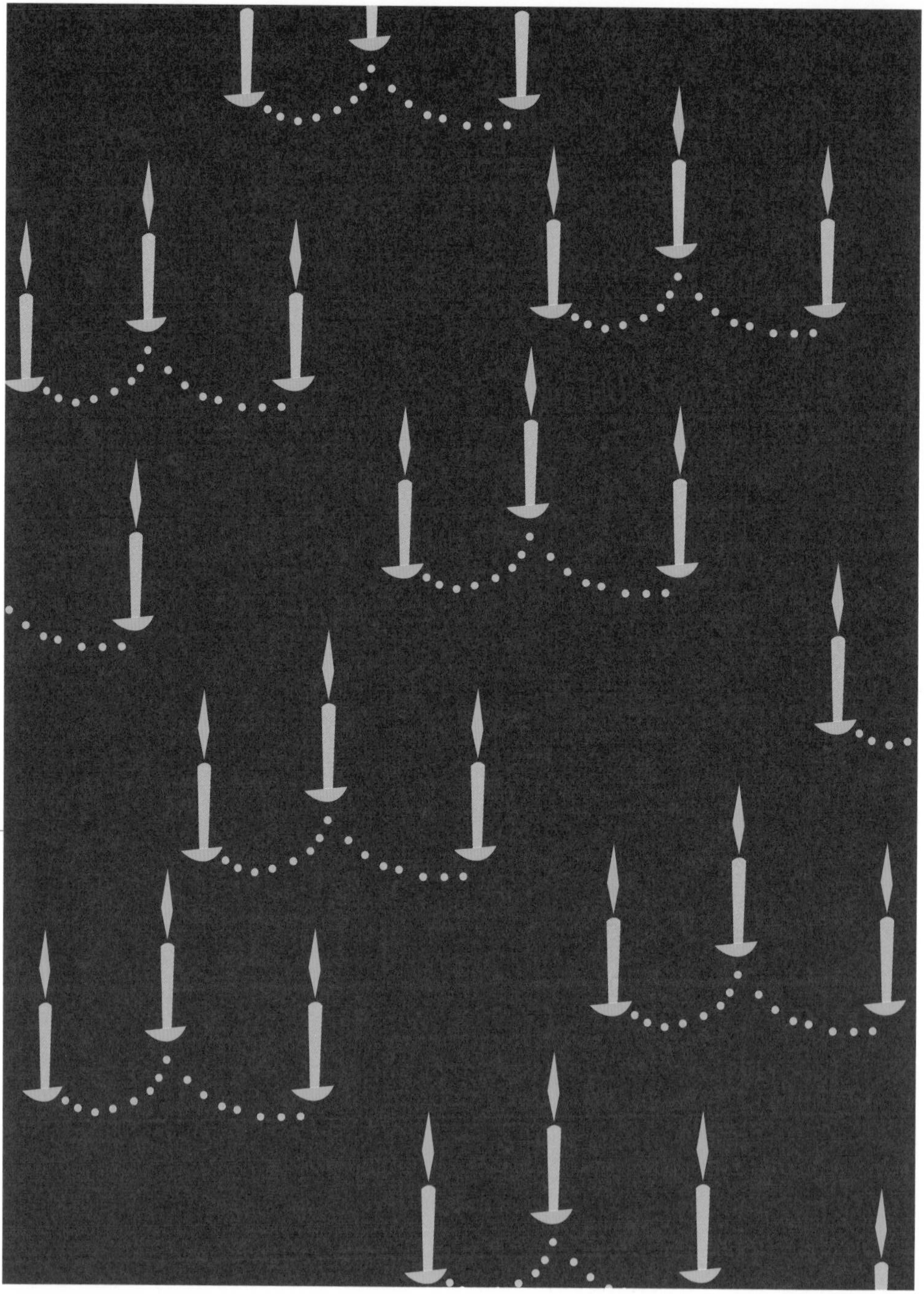

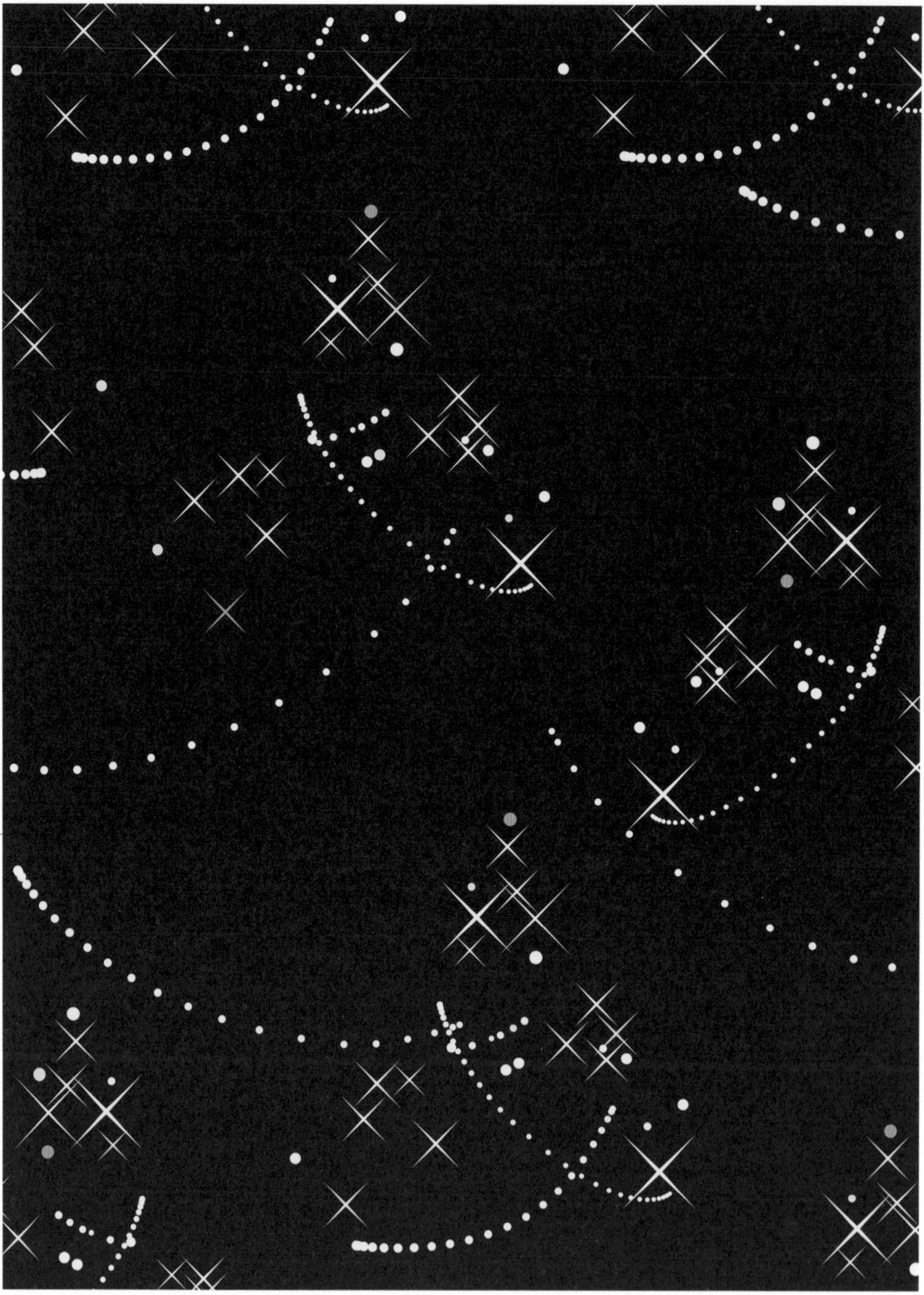

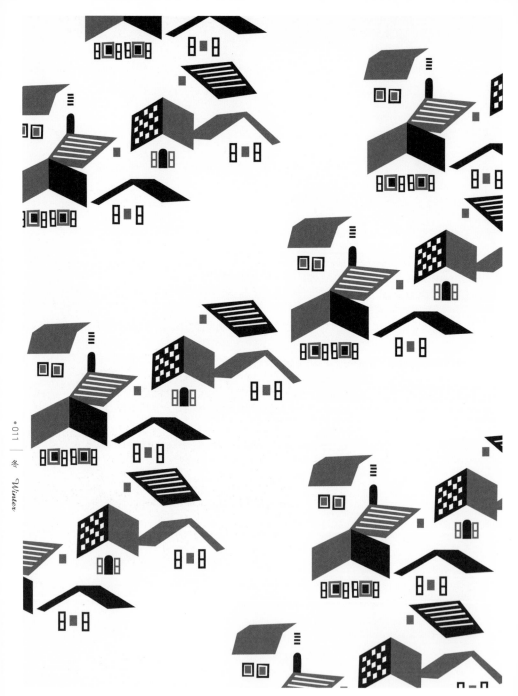

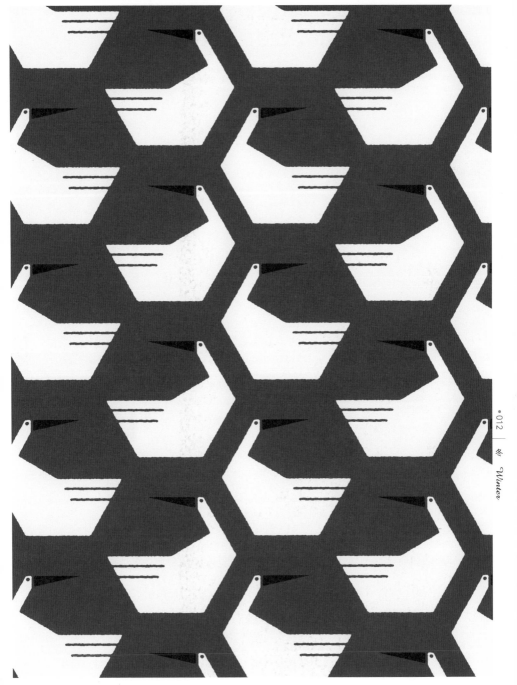

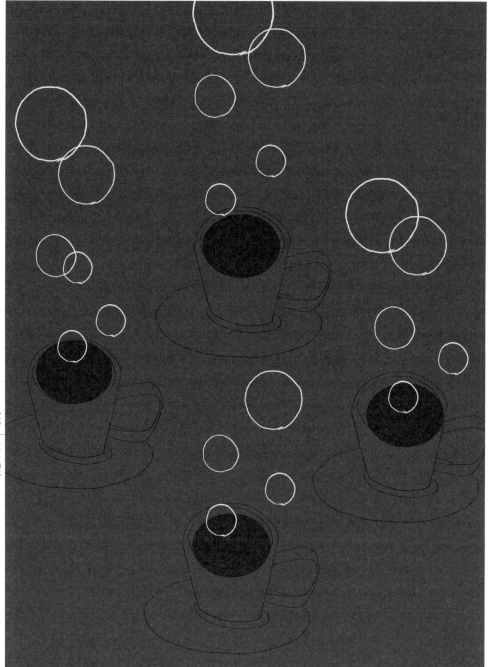

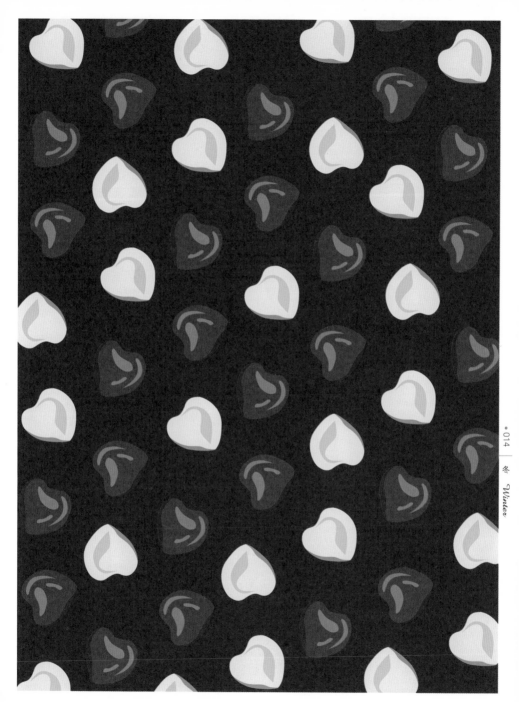

•025 | 冬 Winter

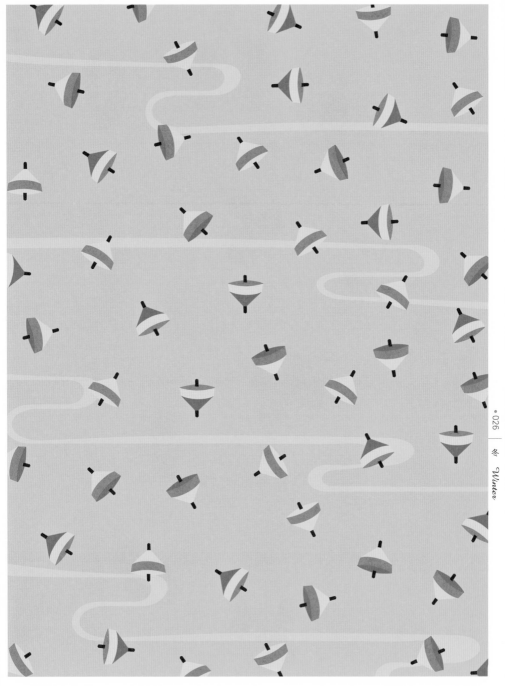

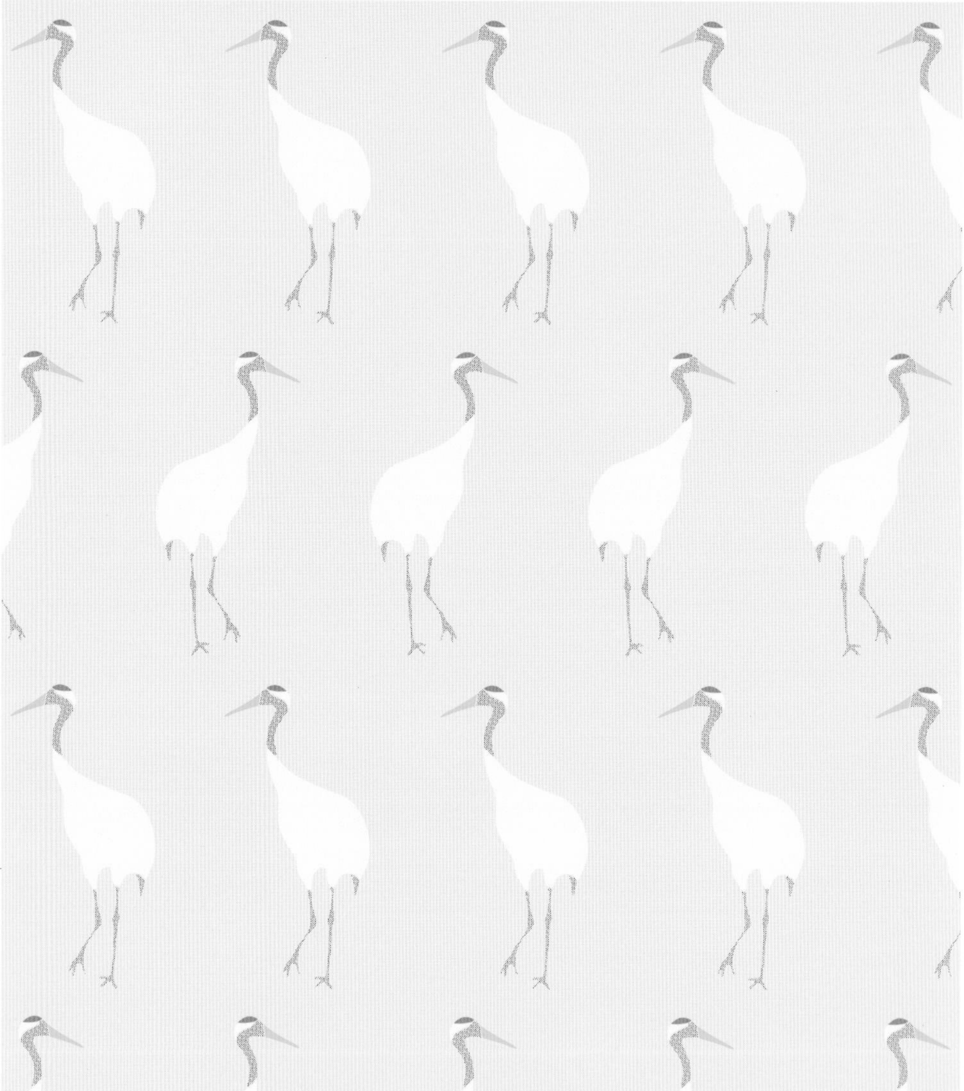

• 031 | 冬 Winter

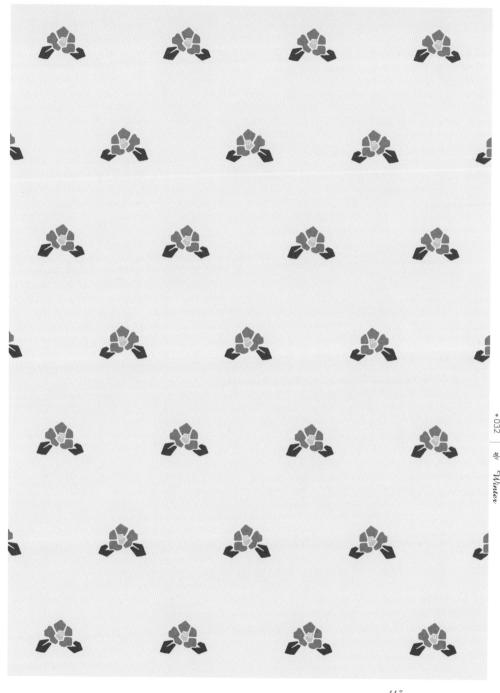

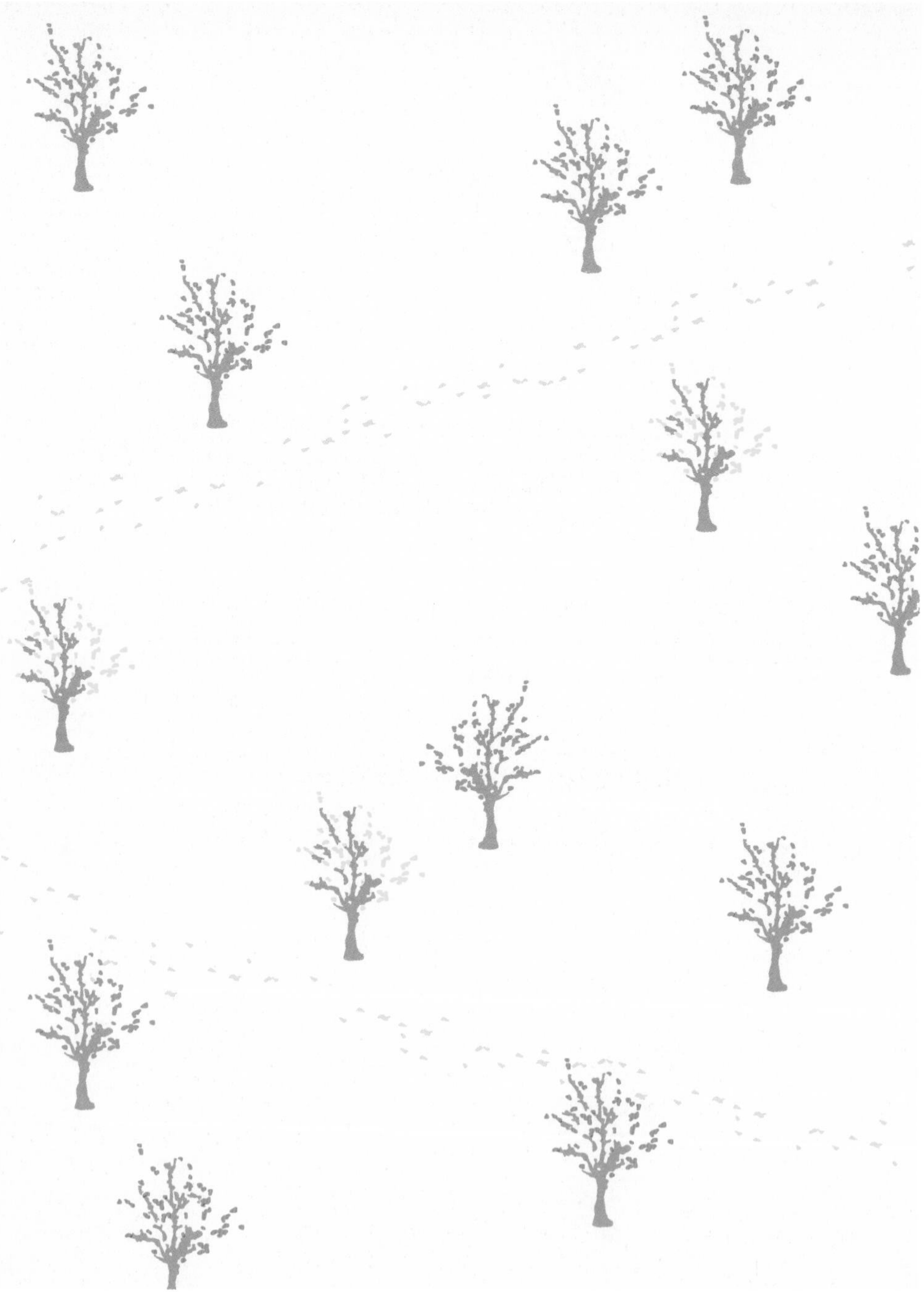

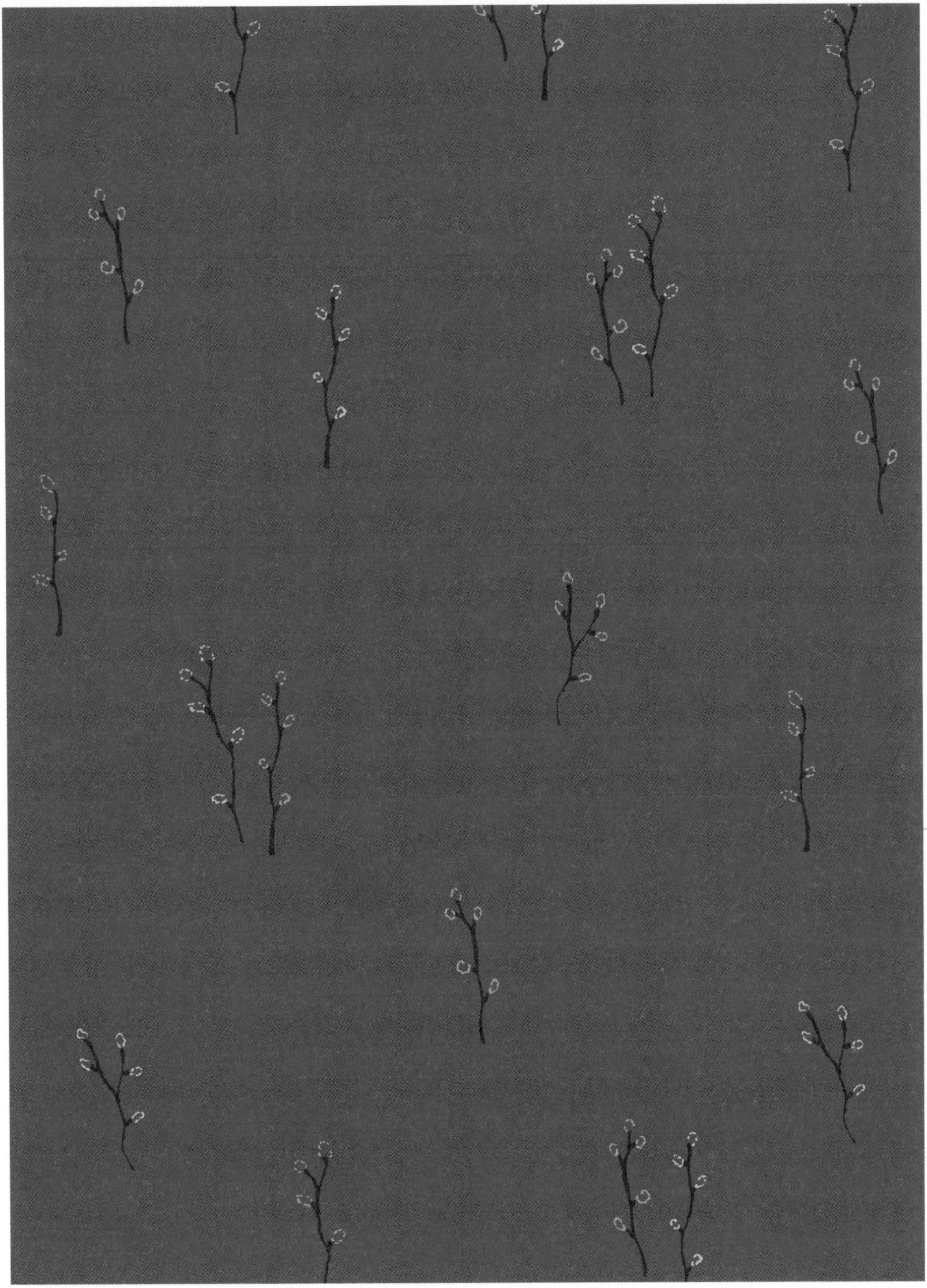

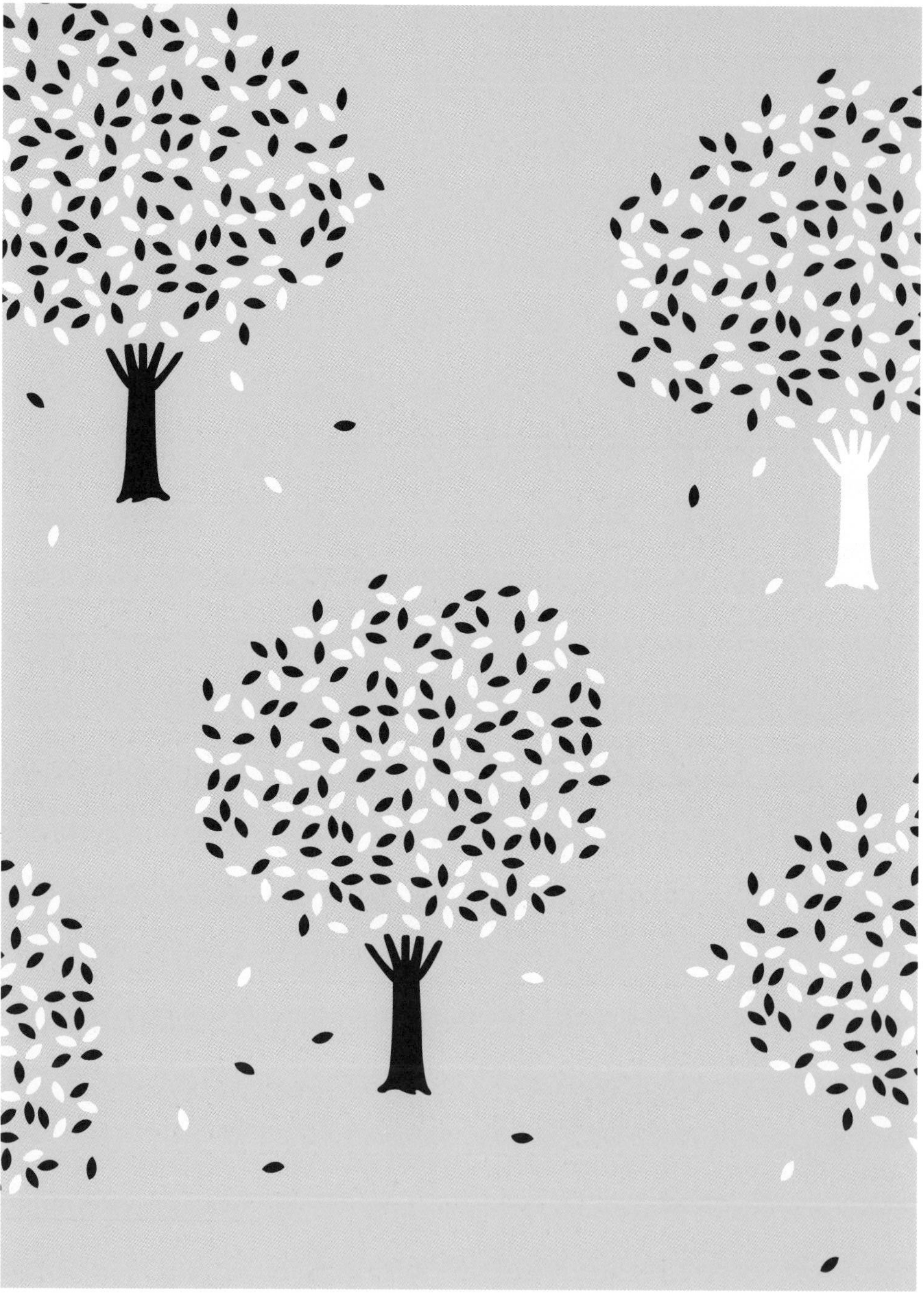

• 035 | 冬 Winter

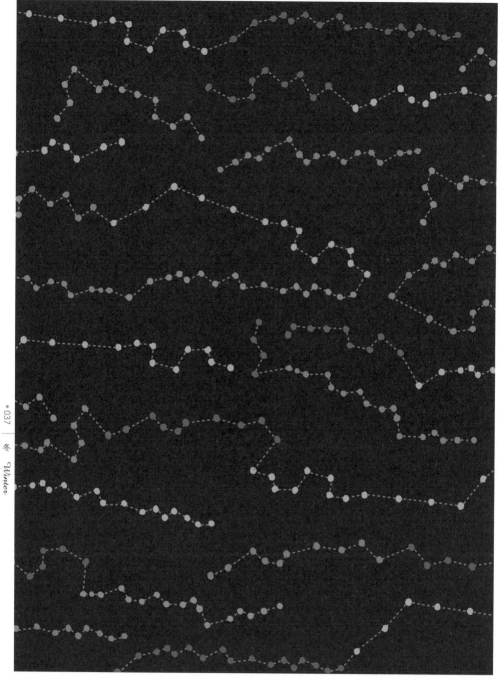

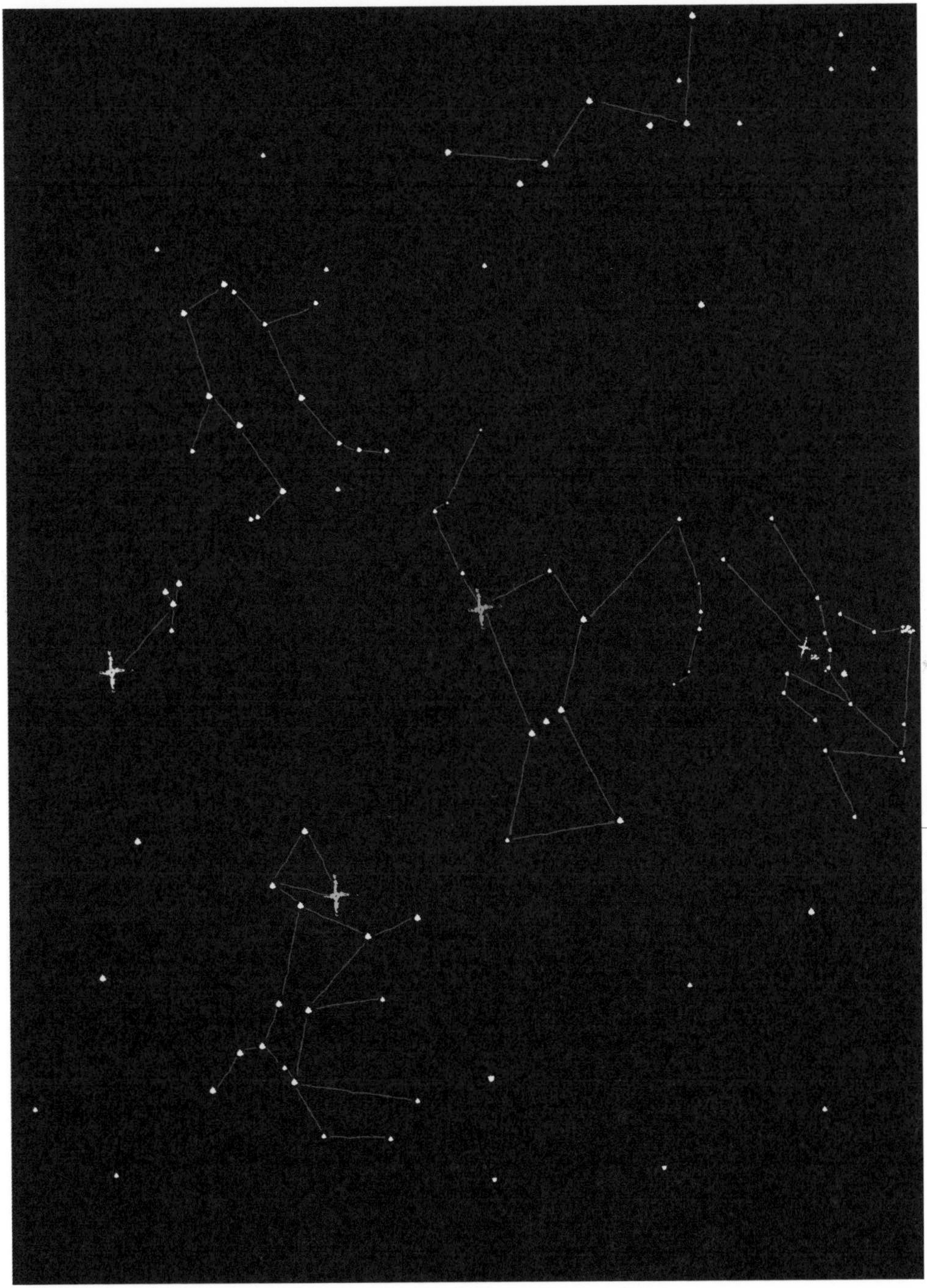

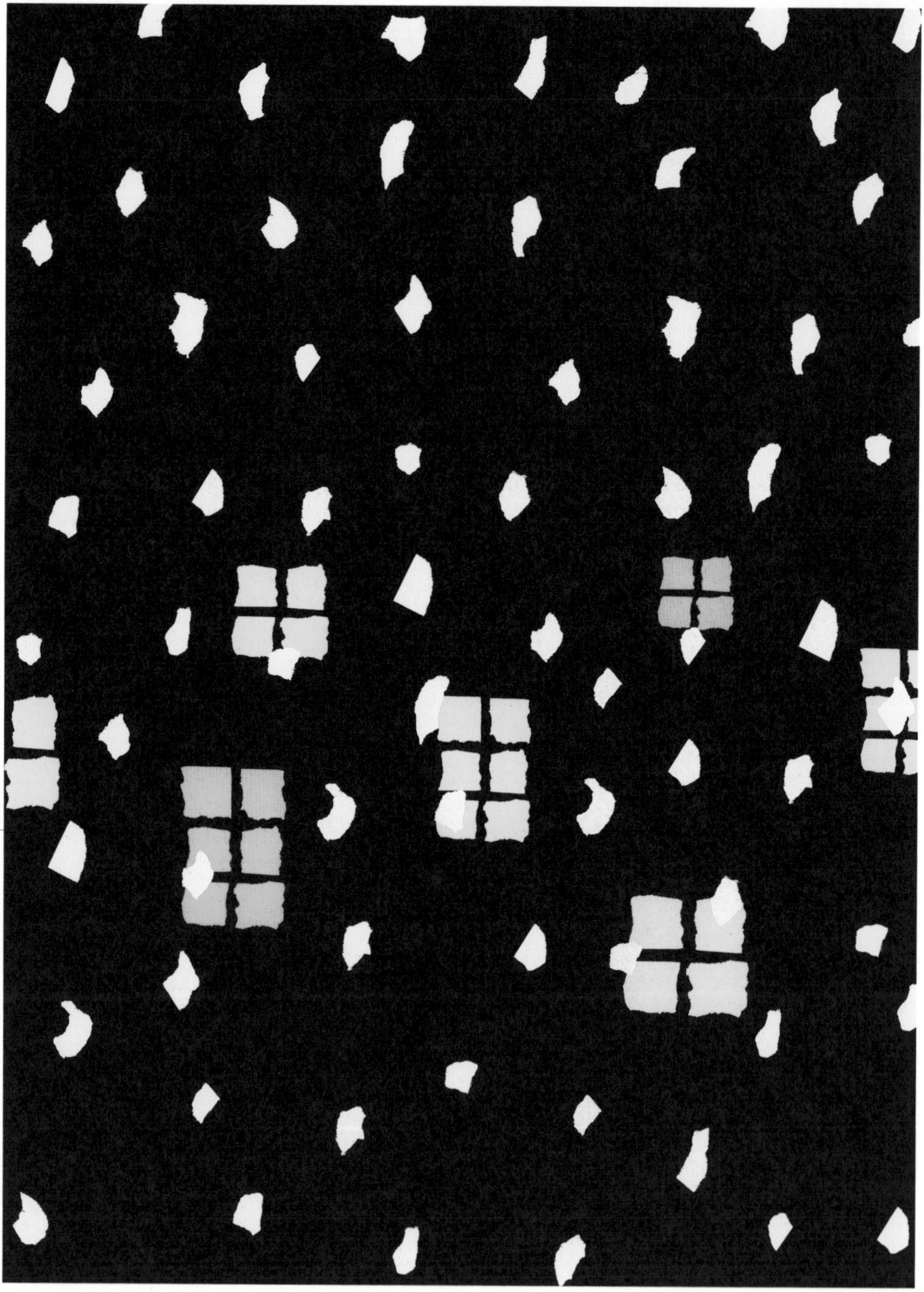

039 冬 Winter

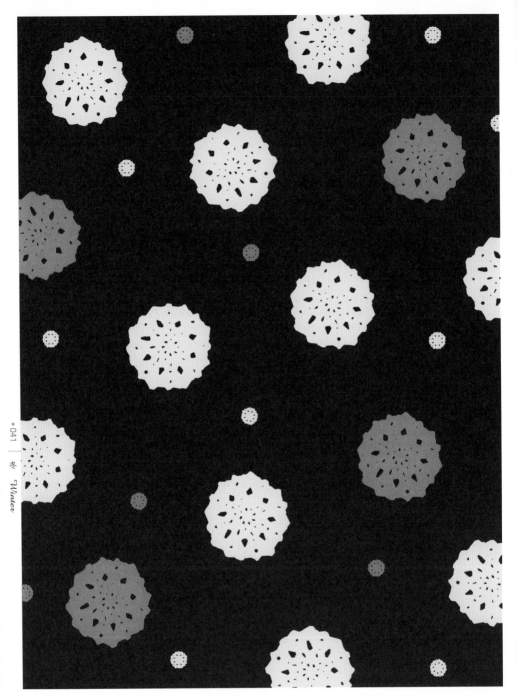

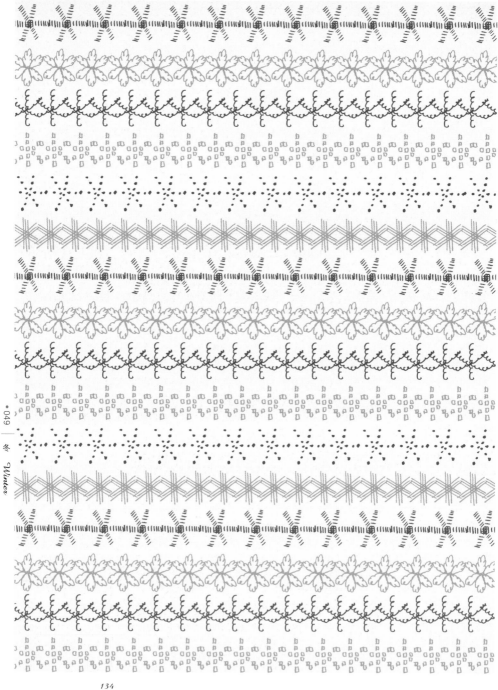

冬 *Winter*

134

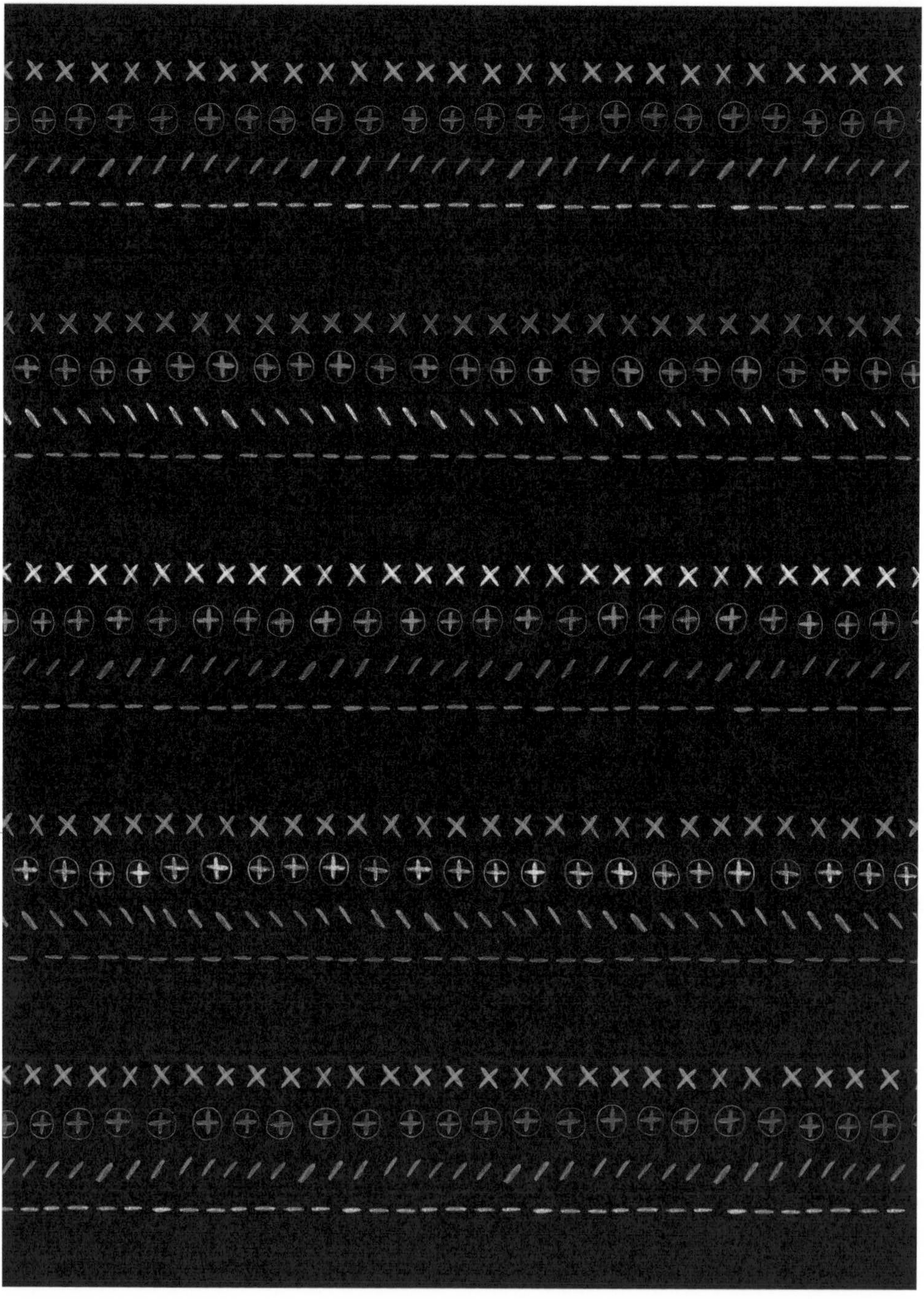

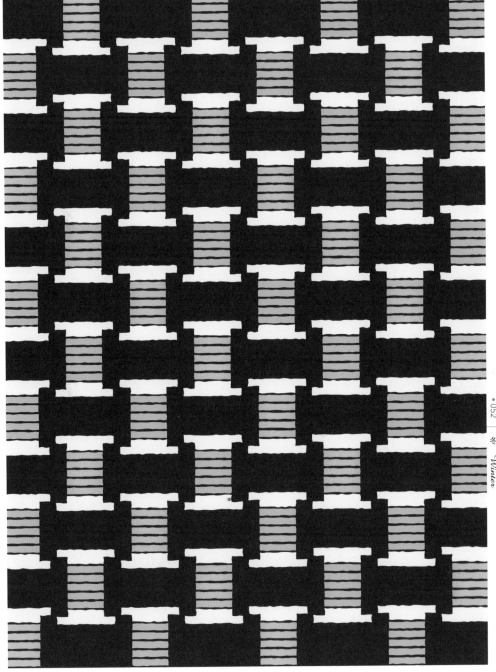

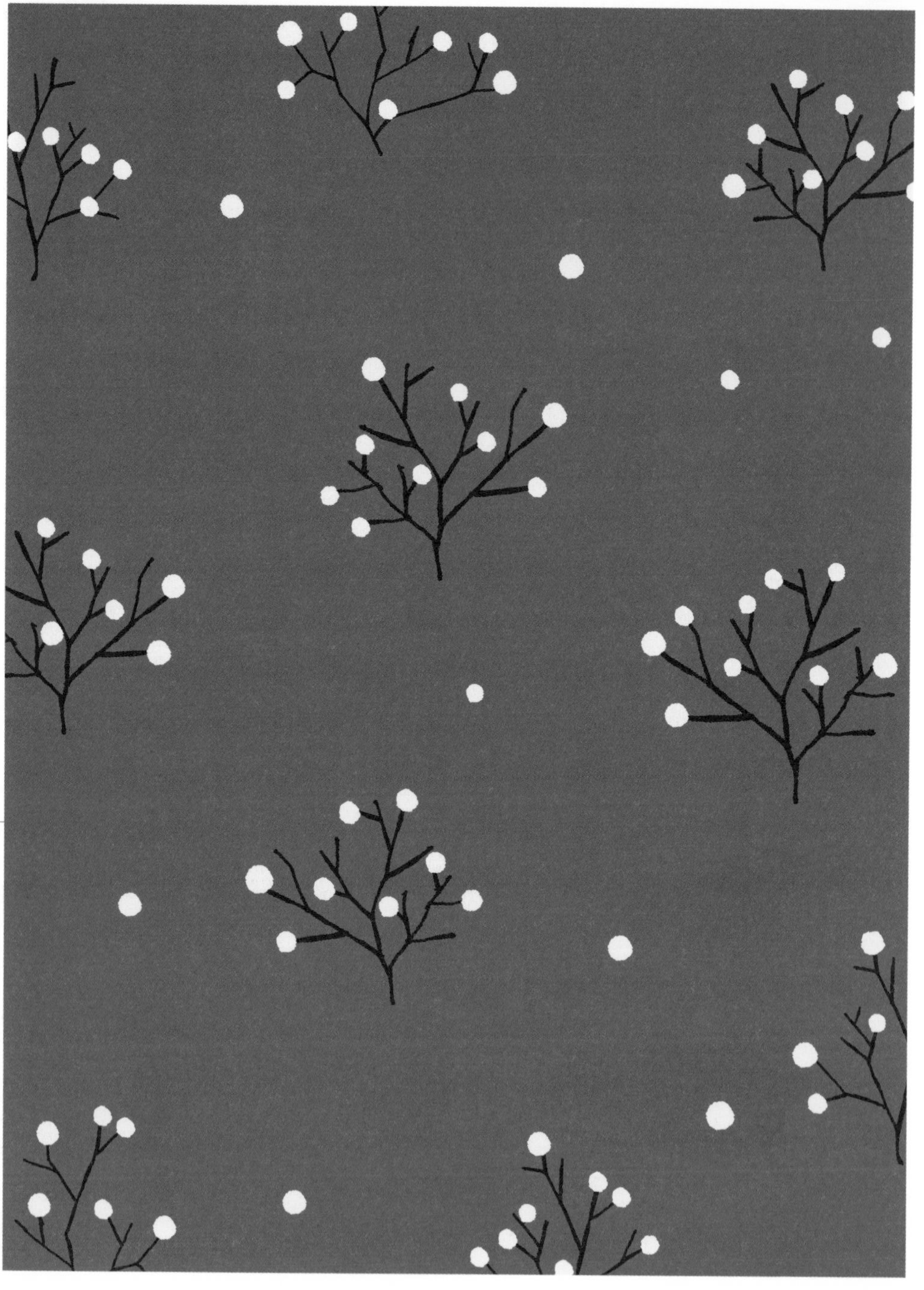

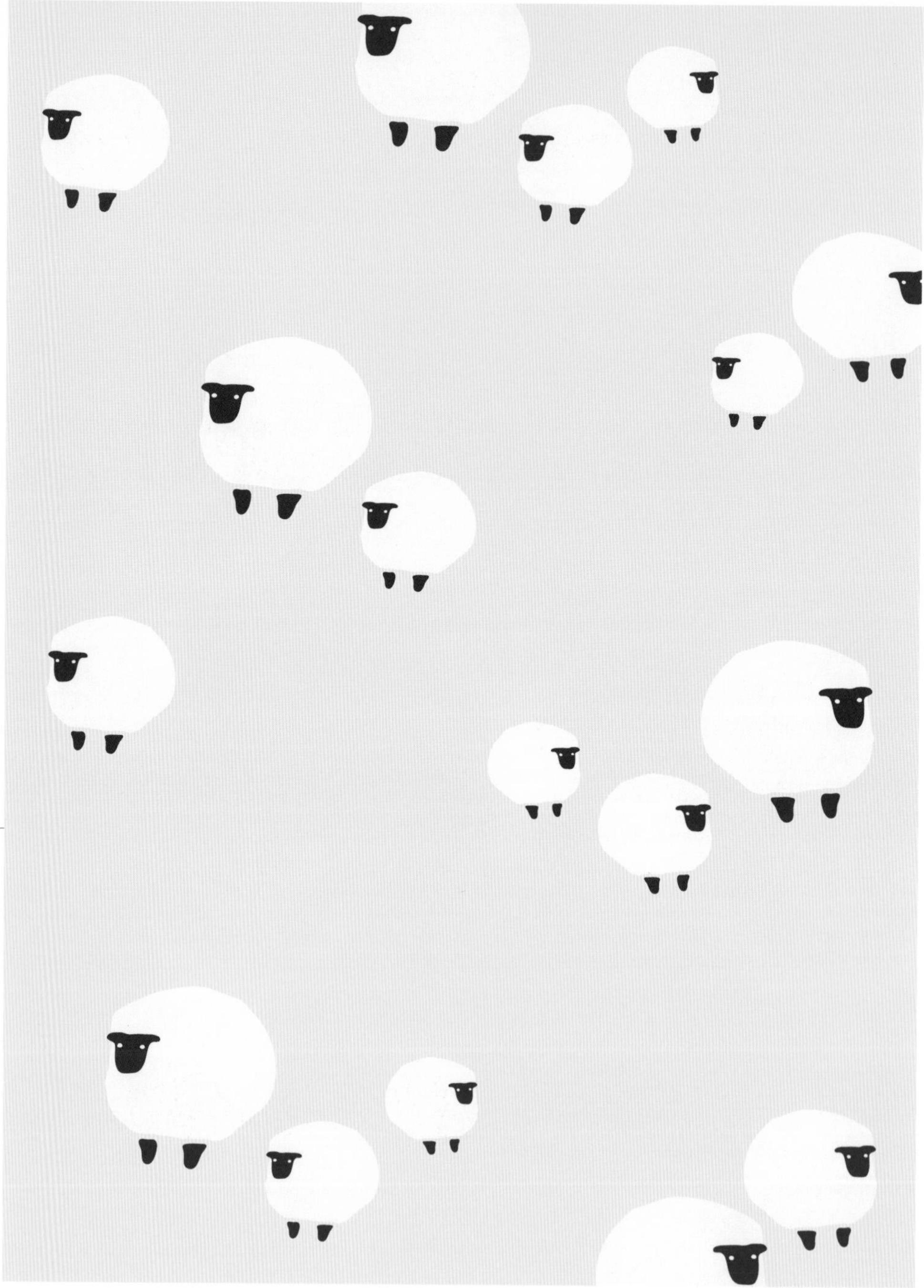

•055 | 冬 Winter

142

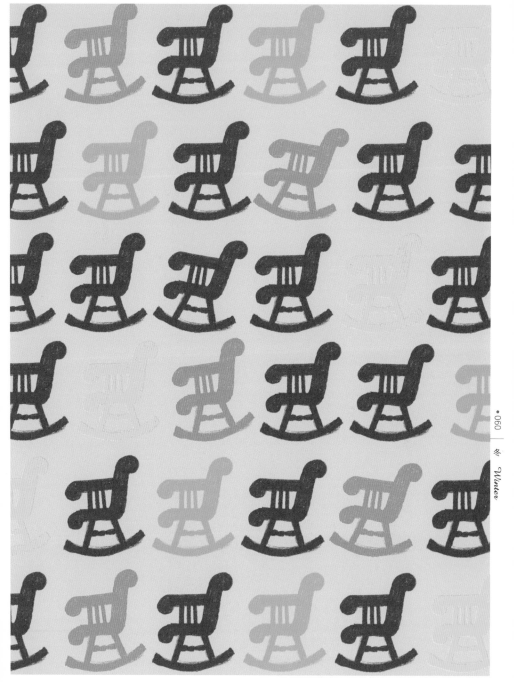

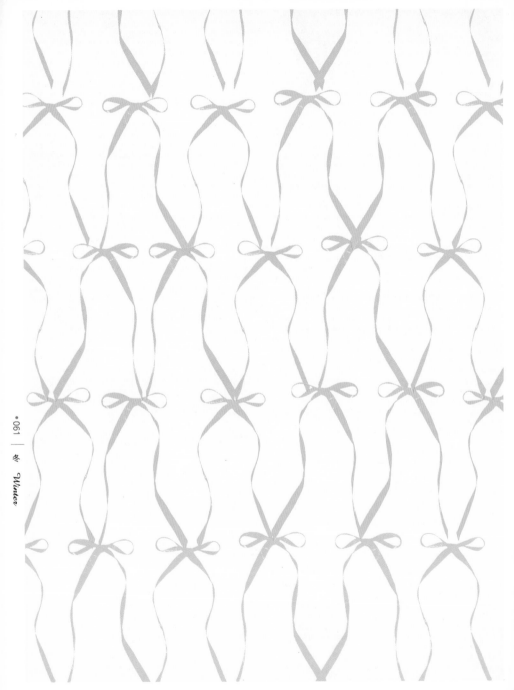

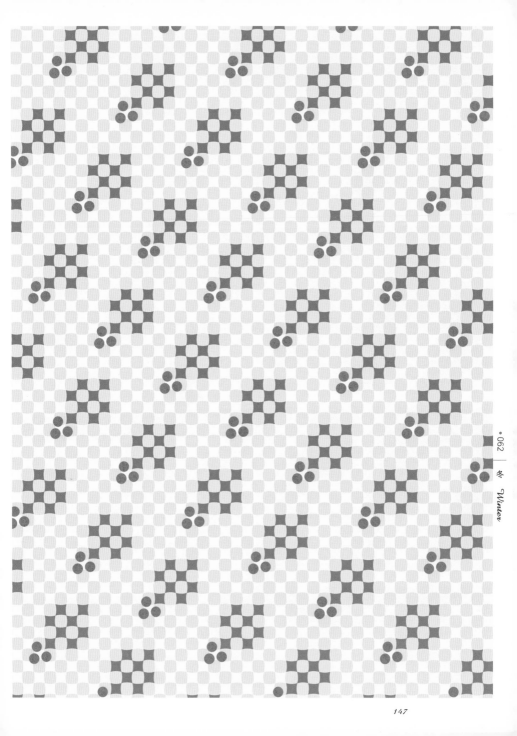

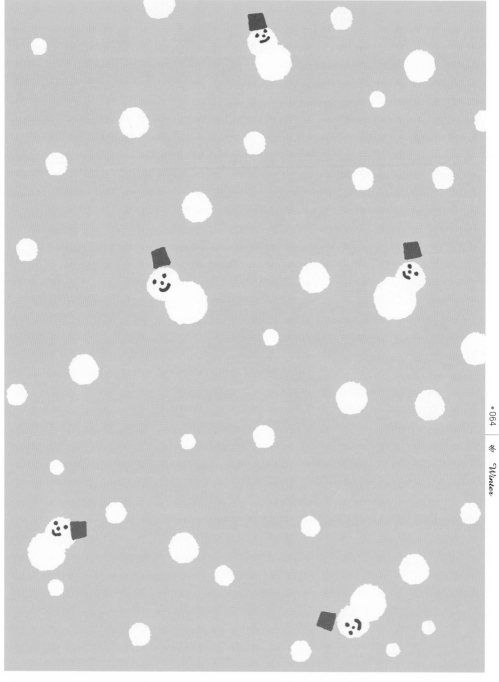

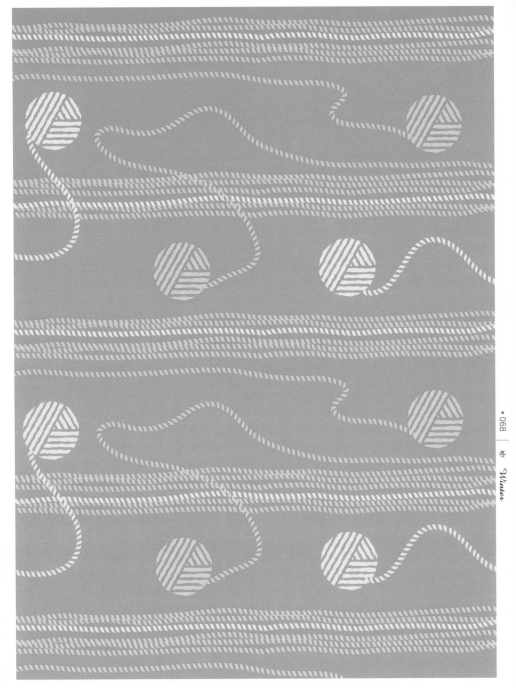

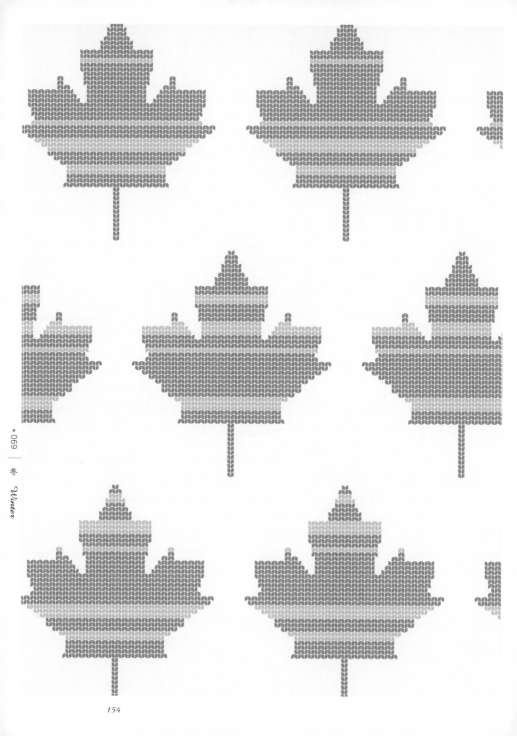

パターンの使い方

(Photoshop & Illustrator)

Petit Pattern Book

how to use patterns

はじめる前に

○注意すること

● CD-ROMをご使用になる前に、必ずP.175の使用許諾をお読みください。

● 本書では、Mac OS X（10.4.5）、Adobe Photoshop CS2、Adobe Illustrator CS2を用いて解説しています。
Windows XP Professional SP1でも動作確認済みですが、環境が異なる場合や、操作方法が分からないときは、
OSやソフトウェアに則した、お手持ちの説明書をお読みください。

● 「パターンをつかってつくるもの」（P.164-169）では、Illustratorとプリンタを使用します。

○準備

まずはCD-ROMをセットして、「Autumn-Winter」
フォルダを開きます。必要なデータをピックアップし
てデスクトップにコピーしましょう。
「Autumn-Winter」フォルダを開くと、「JPEG」と
「EPS」と「Template」という3つのフォルダが入っ
ています。「Template」フォルダに入っているデー
タは、P.164以降で使うサンプルデータです。

Mac

Win

○データの種類

掲載したすべてのパターンには、それぞれJPEGとEPSの2つの形式でファイルを用意しています。
（EPSファイルは、Illustratorのバージョン8.0で保存しています）

JPEG

＊JPEGファイルとして収録したのは、350dpi（商業
印刷に耐え得る解像度）に設定したときに、ほぼA5
サイズの印刷面積を持つビットマップ画像。「Adobe
Photoshop」をはじめとするビットマップ系のソフトウ
ェアで編集できるほか、多くのソフトウェアで扱うこ
とが可能です。

EPS

＊EPSファイルとして収録したのは、拡大縮小を行っ
ても画質が劣化しない、ベクトル画像。ドロー系のソ
フトウェア「Adobe Illustrator」でファイルを開くと、
自在にカスタマイズできます（ビットマップ系のソフトウ
ェア「Adobe Photoshop」で開くと、「ラスタライズ」
という工程を経て、ビットマップイメージに展開します）。

収録したファイルは、どれもタイリング(タイルのように敷き詰めること)が可能な、パターン(繰り返し模様)になっています。PhotoshopやIllustratorといったグラフィックソフトウェアで、パターンを登録する機能を使うと、繰り返し模様を一瞬にして好きなだけ、タイリングできます。いずれのソフトウェアでも「塗り」の設定を用いることから、本書ではこれを「パターンで塗る」と呼びます。

パターンで塗るのは初めて、という人に向けて、ここではPhotoshopとIllustratorを用いて、その設定方法を中心に説明していきます。

○データを開く

Photoshop

「ファイル」メニューから「開く」を選択し、パターンファイル(ここではJPEGファイル)を開きます。

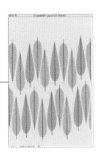

Illustrator

「ファイル」メニューから「開く」を選択し、パターンファイル(ここではEPSファイル)を開きます。選んだパターンがページ中央に表れます。

パターンで塗る
tiling

「Photoshop」編

1. パターンを登録する

好きなパターンファイルを選んで Photoshop で開き
ます。「選択範囲」メニューから「すべてを選択」を選ん
でパターン全体を選択し、「編集」メニューから「パター
ン定義」を選びます。パターンをいつでも使えるように、
分かりやすい名前をつけておきます。

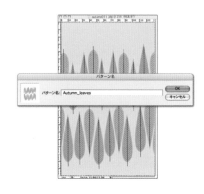

2. 登録したパターンを選ぶ

「ファイル」メニューから「新規」を選んで、パターンで塗
りたい空白の画像ファイルを作成します。ツールバーの
塗りつぶしツールをダブルクリックし、オプションで「パタ
ーン」を選ぶと、先ほど定義したパターンが選択できる
ようになります。

3. パターンで塗る

塗りつぶしツールで画像上の適当な箇所をクリックして、
パターンで塗りつぶします。

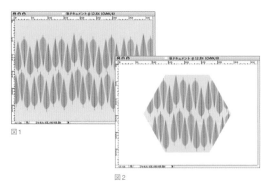

図1

図2

*図1は、A3サイズの空白のファイル
を塗りつぶしたものです。図2のよう
にあらかじめ選択ツールで塗りつぶ
す範囲や形を選択しておくと、パター
ンで選択範囲内のみを塗りつぶすこ
とができます。

パターンで塗る
tiling

「Illustrator」編

1. パターンを登録する

好きなパターンファイルを選んで Illustrator で開きます。「選択」メニューから「すべてを選択」でパターン全体を選択し、「編集」メニューから「コピー」を選ぶとパターンがコピーされます。

「ファイル」メニューから「新規」で空白のドキュメントを作成し、「編集」メニューから「ペースト」を選んでパターンをペーストします。パターン全体が選択された状態のまま、「編集」→「パターン設定」を選んで新規スウォッチを作成し、パターンをいつでも使えるように、分かりやすい名前をつけておきます。

2. 登録したパターンを選ぶ

登録が終わったら、ペーストしたパターンが必要なくなるので、パターン全体が選択された状態のまま、「編集」メニューから「消去」を選んで消します。

「ウインドウ」メニューから「スウォッチ」を選び、スウォッチパレットを表示します。スウォッチパレット内に新たに作成したパターンスウォッチが登録されているので、クリックします。

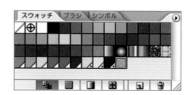

3. パターンで塗る

パターンで塗るオブジェクトを作成します。

図1

図2

＊図1は、長方形ツールで四角形を描いたものです。図2のように他のドローツールで、パターンで塗りつぶされた複雑なオブジェクトを描くこともできます。

番外編 1

「Illustrator」をつかってパターンの色を変える

Step ❶

Illustratorで EPSファイルを開き、「ウインドウ」メニュー
から「スウォッチ」を選択して、スウォッチパレットを表示し
ます。続いて、変更したい色のスウォッチをダブルクリッ
クして、「スウォッチオプション」を表示します。

＊収録された EPSファイルのほとんどは、色や形ごとにレイ
ヤー分けされています。それぞれのレイヤーの順番を入れ替
えたり、非表示にしたり、いろいろなアレンジが可能になって
います。

Step ❷

「スウォッチオプション」上にあるカラーパレットでCMYK
を好きな色に変更します。その際「プレビュー」にチェッ
クを入れておくと、色がパターンにすぐに反映されるので
便利です。色が決定したら「OK」をクリックします。

＊Illustratorで開いた EPSファイルは、サイズを変えたり、
形を変えたり、要素を足したり引いたりと、自由自在。でも、
加工したパターンをスウォッチに登録して使いたい場合は、
タイリングで繋がる部分の四辺のアートワークを、加工で崩
してしまわないよう気を付けましょう。

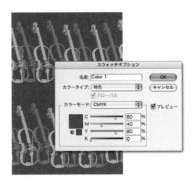

Step ❸

1〜2を繰り返して、オリジナルパターンの出来上がり。
別名で保存しておきましょう。

＊Photoshopで開いた JPEGファイルの色を変更すること
も可能ですが、複雑な輪郭で描かれたパターンは、塗りつ
ぶしツールできれいに色を変更できないことがあります。
そういった場合には、「イメージ」メニューから「色調補正」
→「カラーバランス」もしくは「色相・彩度」で色味を調整す
ることができます。同じパターンの EPSファイルをまずは
Illustratorで開いて色を変更し、別名で JPEG保存したも
のを、次に Photoshopで開いて使う方法もあります。

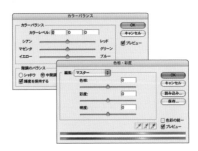

番外編 2

パターンをデスクトップの壁紙にする

Step ❶

Photoshopで壁紙に設定したいパターンのJPEGファ
イルを開いて、「イメージ」メニューから「画像解像度」を
選択し、モニタ表示に充分な「72dpi」に解像度を設定
し直して、別名で保存します。

Step ❷

- for Mac -

Macでは、「アップル」メニューから「システム環境設
定」→「デスクトップとスクリーンセーバ」を選択します。
「フォルダを選択」から先ほど別名で保存したファイルを
指定し、「タイル状に配置」にすると、デスクトップにパ
ターンが表示されます。

- for Windows -

Windowsでは、「コントロールパネル」で「画面」を選択
し、「画面のプロパティ」を開きます（デスクトップ上で右
クリックして選択することもできます）。「デスクトップ」
から先ほど別名で保存したファイルを指定し、「並べて表
示」にすると、デスクトップにパターンが表示されます。

and more !

パターンをウェブサイトの背景にする

上のStep ❶で「72dpi」に解像度を設定し直したデータは、
ホームページの背景にも使えます。
この際にはJPEGファイルを、写真以外のアートワークの保
存に適した、GIF形式に置き換えることをおすすめします。

ペーパーオーナメントをつくる

ゆらゆら揺れるオーナメントは、ツリーや窓辺に下げて。
さり気ないインテリアとしてはもちろん、あちこちに飾って、
クリスマスを迎える準備を始めるのも楽しいですね。

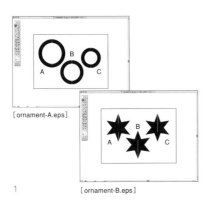

[ornament-A.eps]

[ornament-B.eps]

1

2

3

○用意するもの

印刷用紙、ボール紙、カッター、カッターマット、スプレーのり（なければ液状のりやスティックのり）、目打ち（なければ安全ピンなど）

1. 台紙データを開く

付属CD-ROMの「Template」フォルダには、オーナメント用の台紙データが2種類入っています。「ornament-A.eps」は円形オーナメント、「ornament-B.eps」は星形オーナメントのデータです。作りたいほうのデータをデスクトップにコピーし、Illustratorで開きます。

2. パターンで塗る

次に、使いたいパターンを「スウォッチ」に登録します（P.161参照）。次に、選択ツールで1で開いたドキュメント上のオブジェクトを選択し、オブジェクトの塗りに先ほど登録したパターンを設定します。

3. プリントする

プリンタに印刷用紙をセットし、プリントします。

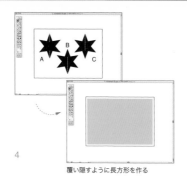

4

覆い隠すように長方形を作る

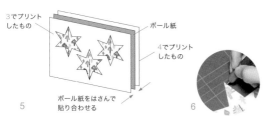

3でプリント
したもの

ボール紙

4でプリント
したもの

5

ボール紙をはさんで
貼り合わせる

6

穴を開ける

[ornament-A]

B   A

①BをAの中に入れ込み、凹凸をかみ合わせる

C   A

②CをBの中に入れ込み、凹凸をかみ合わせて組み立てる

[ornament-B]

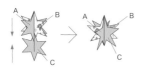

B

A

①Aの切り込みをBの切り込みに合わせて、差し込む

A   B

C

7   ②Cを図のような向きにして、差し込む

4. 長方形を描いて塗る

続いて、オーナメントの各パーツの裏面を作ります。「長方形ツール」を選んで、2のパターンで塗ったオブジェクトの全体を覆い隠すように、大きな長方形を作り、プリントします（長方形はオブジェクトよりひとまわり大きめにしておきましょう）。色は、2で塗ったパターンとの組み合わせや仕上がりをイメージして塗りましょう。また、パターン同士を組み合わせても良いでしょう。

5. ボール紙をはさんで接着する

3と4でプリントした用紙でボール紙をはさみ、スプレーのりで貼り合わせます。

6. カットして穴を開ける

パターンの境界線に沿って各パーツをカットし、切り込み線に沿って切り込みを入れます。糸を通す部分は、目打ちを使って穴を開けておきます。

7. 組み立てて糸を通す

図の手順で組み立てます。最後に、糸を吊るしたい長さにカットし、穴に通せば完成です。

出来上がり！

パターンや色の組み合わせを工夫して、いろいろな種類を作ってみましょう。

ティーコゼーをつくる

飲み物をあたたかいまま保ってくれる、
冬のテーブルには欠かせないティーコゼー。
季節のパターンで手作りすると、お茶の時間が楽しみに。

1　[teacozy-outside.eps]

※今回制作するティーコゼーは、幅18cm×奥行き11cm×高さ13cm程度のポットに合わせた大きさになっています。

○用意するもの

専用布用紙(外布用2枚)、キルティング地(内布用)、リボン(幅2.5cm×長さ10cm程度)、ミシン(なければ手縫いでも可)、縫い針、糸、チャコペン、はさみ、印刷用紙

1. 台紙データを開く

付属CD-ROMの「Template」フォルダの中にある「teacozy-outside.eps」をデスクトップにコピーし、Illustratorで開きます。

2

2. パターンで塗る

次に、使いたいパターンを「スウォッチ」に登録します(P.161参照)。選択ツールを選び、ドキュメント上のオブジェクトを選択します。選択したオブジェクトの塗りに、先ほど登録したパターンを設定します。内布との組み合わせや、仕上がりをイメージしてパターンを選びましょう。

3. 専用布用紙にプリントしてカットする

プリンタに専用布用紙をセットしてプリントします。外布は2枚の布を縫い合わせて仕上げるので、同じものを2枚プリントします。今回使用している用紙は裏面にPETフィルムが貼られたタイプのものです。(プリントの際の細かな設定は、各製品に記載されている注意事項に従って設定してください)。プリントが終わったら、境界線に沿って余白部分をカットし、裏に貼られているPETフィルムをはがします。

3

4 [teacozy-inside.eps]

チャコペンで印を付けて、キルティング
地をカットする

4. 内布をカットする

付属CD-ROMの「Template」フォルダの中にある「teacozy-inside.eps」をデスクトップにコピーします。Illustratorで開き、印刷用紙にプリントして切り抜きます。これを型紙にして、内布用のキルティング地をカットします。内布も外布と同様に2枚作ります。

内布は最後に余った部分を表に返して見せるため、外布に比べ5cmほど縦が長くなっています。

5. 縫製する

外布は、表面が内側にくるように2枚を重ね合わせ、図のようにリボンをはさみ込んで、端から5mm程度内側を縫い合わせます。縫い終わったら表に返します。内布も、表面が内側にくるように2枚を重ね合わせ、返し口を残しながら5mm程度内側を縫い合わせます。

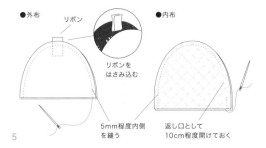

●外布

リボン

リボンを
はさみ込む

●内布

5mm程度内側
を縫う

返し口として
10cm程度開けておく

5

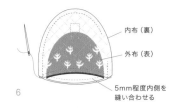

内布（裏）

外布（表）

5mm程度内側を
縫い合わせる

6

6. 口を合わせて縫う

袋状になった内布の中に外布を入れ、図のように口の部分を合わせて縫います。

7. 表に返し、余った部分をかぶせる

①まず、返し口から表に返します。②図のような状態になったら、返し口を縫って閉じます。③内布を内側に入れ、図のように余った部分を折り、上にかぶせます。④外布と内布の境い目に落しミシンをかけ、かぶせた内布を固定したら完成です。

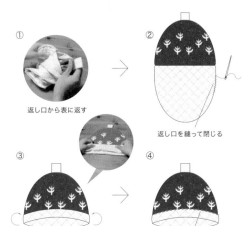

①

返し口から表に返す

②

返し口を縫って閉じる

③

余った部分を折って
上にかぶせる

④

境い目に落しミシン
をかける

7

出来上がり！

お揃いの柄でポットマットやコースターなどを作ってもかわいいですね。

パズルカレンダーをつくる

六角形の可愛くてふしぎなカレンダー。
オブジェのように棚に飾ったり、たたんで持ち歩いたり、
折り方を変えるだけでパズルのように楽しめます。

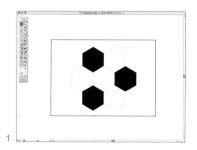

1

○用意するもの

画用紙、印刷用紙、カッター、カッターマット、スプレーのり（なければ液状のりやスティックのり）、定規、鉄筆（なければインクの切れたボールペンや芯を出さないシャープペンシルなどでも可）

1. 台紙データを開く

付属CD-ROMの「Template」フォルダの中にある「calendar.eps」をデスクトップにコピーし、Illustratorで開きます。

2. パターンを使ってデザインする

一つの六角カレンダーは片面3ヶ月、両面合わせて6ヶ月分のカレンダーになります。先に片面3ヶ月分を作成します。

まず、黒く塗られていない六角形オブジェクトに、月、日、曜日といったカレンダーの要素をデザインしていきます（「Template」フォルダの中にある「calendar2008.eps」には、2008年度のカレンダーデータが入っています。これを利用すると簡単に作成できます）。

次に、黒く塗りつぶされた六角形オブジェクトをパターンで塗っていきます。それぞれの月に合わせたイメージでパターンを選び、「スウォッチ」に登録して（P.161参照）、選択したオブジェクトの塗りにパターンを設定します。その際、右側にカレンダー／左側にその月をイメージさせるパターン、という並びになるよう注意しましょう。

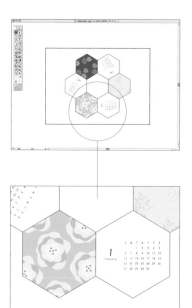

2

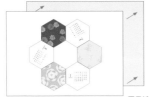

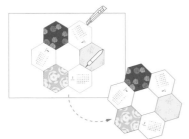

画用紙に貼る

3

3. プリントして画用紙に貼る

デザインが完成したらプリンタに印刷用紙をセットし、プリントします。

プリントした用紙の裏にしっかりとスプレーのりを吹き付け、画用紙に貼ります。

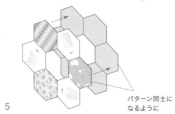

4

4. 折りすじを入れてカットする

まず、図のようにパターンとカレンダーの境界線に、鉛筆で折りすじを入れます。次に、外側と内側の境界線に沿ってカットしていきます。これで片面が完成です。

5

パターン同士になるように

5. 残りの3ヶ月分を作る

もう一度1〜2の手順を繰り返し、残りの3ヶ月分を作ります。今度はプリントした用紙を先にカットします。次に4で作ったものを裏面にのりでしっかりと貼り付けます。このとき、表と裏でパターンの面とカレンダーの面が同じ場所に揃うよう、注意して貼り合わせましょう。

6

山折り

谷折り

6. 折りすじに合わせて折る

最後に図のように、4で入れた折りすじに合わせて折ります。

出来上がり!

折り方次第でいろいろと楽しめます。

秋・冬
Autumn & Winter

→ 秋 *Autumn*

°001
autumn001

°002
autumn002

°003
autumn003

°004
autumn004

°005
autumn005

°006
autumn006

°007
autumn007

°008
autumn008

°009
autumn009

°010
autumn010

°011
autumn011

°012
autumn012

°013
autumn013

°014
autumn014

°015
autumn015

°016
autumn016

°017
autumn017

°018
autumn018

°019
autumn019

°020
autumn020

°021
autumn021

°022
autumn022

°023
autumn023

°024
autumn024

°025
autumn025

°026
autumn026

°027
autumn027

°028
autumn028

°029
autumn029

°030
autumn030

°031
autumn031

°032
autumn032

°033
autumn033

°034
autumn034

°035
autumn035

°036
autumn036

°037
autumn037

°038
autumn038

°039
autumn039

°040
autumn040

°041
autumn041

°042
autumn042

°043
autumn043

°044
autumn044

°045
autumn045

°046
autumn046

°047
autumn047

°048
autumn048

°049
autumn049

°050
autumn050

°051
autumn051

°052
autumn052

°053
autumn053

°054
autumn054

°055
autumn055

°056
autumn056

°057
autumn057

°058
autumn058

°059
autumn059

°060
autumn060

°061
autumn061

°062
autumn062

°063
autumn063

°064
autumn064

°065
autumn065

°066
autumn066

°067
autumn067

°068
autumn068

°069
autumn069

°070
autumn070

↳ 冬 *Winter*

°001
winter001

°002
winter002

°003
winter003

°004
winter004

°005
winter005

°006
winter006

°007
winter007

°008
winter008

°009
winter009

°010
winter010

011
winter011

012
winter012

013
winter013

014
winter014

015
winter015

016
winter016

017
winter017

018
winter018

019
winter019

020
winter020

021
winter021

022
winter022

023
winter023

024
winter024

025
winter025

026
winter026

027
winter027

028
winter028

029
winter029

030
winter030

031
winter031

032
winter032

033
winter033

034
winter034

035
winter035

036
winter036

037
winter037

038
winter038

039
winter039

040
winter040

*041
winter041

*042
winter042

*043
winter043

*044
winter044

*045
winter045

*046
winter046

*047
winter047

*048
winter048

*049
winter049

*050
winter050

*051
winter051

*052
winter052

*053
winter053

*054
winter054

*055
winter055

*056
winter056

*057
winter057

*058
winter058

*059
winter059

*060
winter060

*061
winter061

*062
winter062

*063
winter063

*064
winter064

*065
winter065

*066
winter066

*067
winter067

*068
winter068

*069
winter069

*070
winter070

『おしゃれなパターン素材集 秋・冬』
付属CD-ROM使用許諾書（ソフトウェアライセンス契約書）

1. ライセンス
1) 株式会社ビー・エヌ・エヌ新社（以下「弊社」という。）は、本製品を購入され、本使用許諾書記載の条件に合意
　されたお客様（以下「ユーザー」という。）に対し、本ソフトウェアを同時に1台のコンピュータ上でのみ使用できる、
　譲渡不能の非独占的権利を許諾します。
2) ユーザーは、2の「制限事由」に該当する場合を除き、本ソフトウェアに含まれる素材を加工・編集し、もしくは
　他の素材と組み合わせるなどして、主に以下のデザインに使用することができます。
　○ WEBなどのデジタルメディア
　○ 店舗の内装、案内表示、レジにおける無料パッケージなどのグラフィックツール
　○ 印刷物として頒布するチラシ、フライヤー、ポスター、DM、カタログ、パンフレットなどの広告・販売促進ツール
　○ 個人制作・個人利用の雑貨、服、グリーティングカード、名刺など
　　（個人的・職業的・商業的用途の利用を認めますが、いずれも非売品のデザインに限ります。個人においても
　　素材を利用した制作物の販売は行えません。次の制限事由をよくお読み下さい。）

2. 制限事由
以下の行為を禁止します。
1) 本ソフトウェアを1台のコンピュータで使用するためのやむを得ぬ場合を除き、本ソフトウェアを複製すること
2) 本使用許諾書に基づくライセンスを他に譲渡し、本製品の貸与もしくはその他の方法で本ソフトウェアを他者
　に使用させること
3) 流通を目的とした商品のデザインに素材を利用すること（書籍や雑誌など、有料の印刷物を含む。）
4) 商品パッケージおよび有料のギフトパッケージに素材を利用すること
5) 素材をブランドイメージとして利用すること（可能性があると判断できるものも含む。）
6) 素材を利用してポストカード、名刺、雑貨などの制作販売または制作サービスを行うこと
7) 素材を利用してインターネットによるダウンロードサービスを行うこと（グリーティングカード・サービスを含む。）
8) 素材をホームページ上で公開する場合に、オリジナルデータがダウンロード可能となる環境を作ること
9) ソフトウェア製品等を製造・販売するために素材を流用すること
10) 素材そのものや素材を用いた制作物について意匠権などの権利を取得すること
11) 素材を公序良俗に反する目的、誹謗・中傷目的で利用すること

※本素材を使用した商業デザインや商品販売等をお考えの際にはご相談に応じます。
　事前に下記までご連絡ください。
　○有限会社ニメートル○九センチグラフィックス（fax：03-3470-2356　e-mail：info@209g.com）

3. 著作権、その他の知的財産権
　本ソフトウェアおよび素材に関する著作権、その他の知的財産権は、弊社または弊社への供給者の排他的財産
　として留保されています。素材を利用した制作物においてユーザーの著作権を明示する場合は、併せてパターン
　の著作権「©2007 2m09cmGRAPHICS, Inc.」を明示してください。

4. 責任の制限
　弊社および弊社への供給者は、請求原因の如何を問わず、本ソフトウェアの使用または使用の不能および素材
　の利用から生じるすべての損害や不利益（利益の逸失およびデータの損壊を含む。）につき、一切責任を負わな
　いものとします。

5. 使用許諾の終了
　ユーザーが本使用許諾書に違反した場合、弊社は、本使用許諾書に基づくユーザーのライセンスを終了させる
　ことができます。

○撮影協力 *Special Thanks*

FORM ASH + BARN

1988年に世田谷でOrange Barn（オレンジバーン）としてスタートし、1997年に南
青山にアッシュコンテンポラリーを設立。2000年に両店舗を統合しFORM ASH＋
BARNとなり、現在に至る。
新築一戸建て、マンションリフォーム、オーダーキッチン、オリジナル家具、etc…。
当初から、無垢材や左官材などを取り入れ、昔から使われている自然素材にこ
だわった家作り、ただ自然素材を使うだけでなく形もシンプルで機能的なもの
作りを追求している。

○tel：03-5775-6412
○fax：03-5775-6413
○e-mail：ash-barn@form-tokyo.com
○web：www.form-tokyo.com

相原 祐子 *Yuko Aihara*

フードコーディネーター
1981年生まれ。芸術大学卒業後、カフェ・レストランなどでスイーツに携わる。
2005年「とりどりの暮らし（ドーナツのススメ）」を自費出版。フードユニット
timid campを結成し、さまざまなイベントに参加。フードスタイリング・レシ
ピ提案・ケータリングなどに取り組み、さまざまな形で「食の楽しさ」を表現し
ている。

○e-mail：aihara_yuko@yahoo.co.jp

Petit Pattern Book

How to use patterns

(Photoshop & Illustrator)

Before you start

○ Notes

- Please read the License Agreement on page 190 before you start.
- The explanation in this book is based on Mac OS X (10.4.5), Adobe Photoshop CS2, and Adobe Illustrator CS2. The functionality has also been verified with Windows XP Professional SP1. If your system is different, or if you have a question concerning the operation of the software, refer to the manuals corresponding to your OS and software.
- In the chapter "Let's use the patterns to make an original article" (p184-189), you will be using Illustrator and your printer.

○ Preparation

Mac

At first, set the attached CD-ROM and open "Autumn-Winter" folder. Pick up the patterns you need and copy them to your desktop.

Open the folder "Autumn-Winter" and you will find three folders: "JPEG" , "EPS" , and "Template". You are going to use the data inside "Template" from p184 as sample data later on.

○ Different kinds of data

All the patterns in the book are prepared in the following two formats:
(EPS files are saved with Illustrator 8.0.)

JPEG

EPS

※In the JPEG file, you will find bitmap images which are printed on the surface of around 148× 210mm at 350 dpi (the resolution suitable for commercial printing). You can edit them with Adobe Photoshop and other bitmap software, and you can use it with many other types of software.

※In the EPS file, you will find vector images, which do not deteriorate when you increase or reduce the size. Open the file with Adobe Illustrator or other drawing software, and you will be able to customize the images freely (When you open the file with bitmap software such as Adobe Photoshop, the image will be developed as a bitmap image after the process called rasterizing).

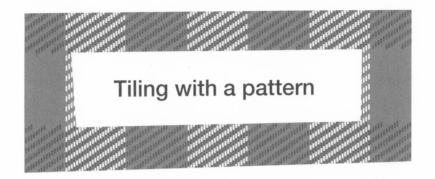

Tiling with a pattern

All the files are repeated patterns which can be tiled. Register patterns in Photoshop, Illustrator or other graphic software, and you can tile one of the repeated patterns in the blink of an eye.

For those people who have never tiled with patterns, we shall explain how to do it using Photoshop and Illustrator, focusing on the settings.

● Open the data

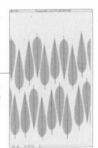

Photoshop

Select "Open" from the "File" menu, and open the pattern file (JPEG file here).

Illustrator

Select "Open" from the "File" menu, and open the pattern file (EPS file here). The pattern chosen will appear in the centre of the screen.

How to tile with

Photoshop

1. Save the pattern

Open your favorite pattern with Photoshop. Select the whole image by choosing "Select" → "All", and select "Edit" → "Define Pattern". Give the pattern an easily recognized name so that you can use it whenever you want.

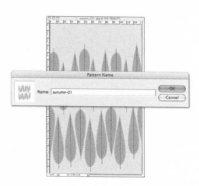

2. Select the saved pattern

Select "File" → "New" and create a blank image file to be filled with the pattern. Double click on Paint Bucket Tool and select "Pattern" from the options, and you are able to choose the pattern you have already defined.

3. Tiling with the pattern

Click on the image with the Paint Bucket Tool and tile the whole image with the pattern.

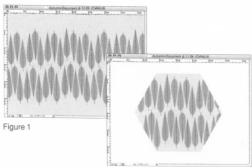

Figure 1

Figure 2

※Figure1 shows a blank 420× 297mm file tiled with a pattern. If you use Select tools to select the part of the image to be tiled, you can tile only the part and the shape you have selected.

How to tile with
Illustrator

1. Save the pattern

Open your favorite pattern with Illustrator. Select the whole image by choosing "Select" → "All", and "Edit"→"Copy" to copy the pattern.

Create a blank document by selecting "File"→ "New", and paste the pattern by selecting "Edit" →"Paste". While the whole pattern is still selected, select "Edit" →"Define Pattern" to create a new swatch and give it an easily recognized name so that you can use it whenever you want.

2. Select the saved pattern

When you have saved the image, delete the pattern you pasted previously, as you do not need it any more. While the whole pattern is still selected, select "Edit"→ "Clear" and the pattern will be deleted.

Select "Window" → "Swatches" to show the swatch pallet. Click the newly registered pattern on the swatch pallet.

3. Tiling with the pattern

Make an object to be tiled with the pattern.

Figure 1

※ Figure 1 shows a rectangular shape drawn with the Rectangular Tool. You can also draw a complicated object tiled with the pattern with other tools, as shown in Figure 2.

Figure 2

Extra 1

How to change the color of a pattern with Illustrator

Step 1

Open the EPS file with Illustrator (see p179). Select "Window" → "Swatches" to show the swatch pallet. Double click the swatch of the color you would like to change to show "Swatch Options".

※Most of the EPS files have different layers for each color and shape: you can arrange the patterns by changing the layer orders or hiding a layer.

Step 2

Modify CMYK on the color pallet on "Swatch Options" to create your own color. You can select the "Preview" option beforehand to show the new color immediately. When you have obtained the color you want, click "OK".

※If you have opened the EPS file with Illustrator, you can modify the pattern any way you like: by changing the size, the shape, adding or taking out an element, etc. On the other hand, if you would like to save the modified pattern in Swatch for future use, avoid breaking the square artwork of its four sides, which would be juxtaposed on the tiling image.

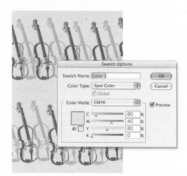

Step 3

Repeat 1-2 and create your own original pattern. Save it under a different name.

※While it is also possible to change the color of the JPEG file with Photoshop using the Paint Bucket Tool, the new color may be fuzzy in some patterns drawn using complicated lines. If this happens, select "Image" →"Adjustments" → "Color Balance" or "Hue/Saturation" to correct the color. Alternatively, open the EPS file of the same pattern with Illustrator, change the color, save as a JPEG file under a different name, and open and use it with Photoshop.

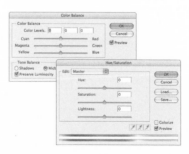

How to use the pattern as a desktop background of your computer

Step 1

Open the JPEG file with Photoshop (see p179), select "Image" → "Image Size". Change the resolution to "72 dpi", the resolution suitable for the monitor, and save it under a new name.

Step 2

-for Mac-

Go to the "Apple" menu and select "System Preferences" → "Desktop & Screen Saver". Select the saved file in Step1 for the desktop background, and choose "Tile" to make the pattern appear on the desktop.

-for Windows-

Go to "Control Panel", and open "Display Properties" (you can also select it by right-clicking your mouse on the desktop). Click the "Desktop" tab, select the saved file in Step1 for the background, and chose "Tile" to show the pattern on the desktop.

Using the pattern for the background of your website

The data at resolution "72 dpi" at Step1 above can also be used as the background of a website.
In this case, it is recommended that you transfer the date to the GIF format, which is suitable for saving artworks other than photos.

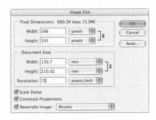

How to make a "paper ornament"

Hang your ornaments to swing on a Christmas tree or by the window. You can decorate your rooms with them and be ready for Christmas.

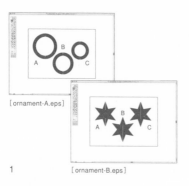

[ornament-A.eps]

1

[ornament-B.eps]

○You will need:

Printing paper, cardboard, cutter, cutting mat, spray glue (if not available use liquid glue or glue stick), punch (or safety pin)

1. Open the mount data

You will find two ornament data in the "Template" folder in the attached CD-ROM: "ornament-A.eps" for the circle ornament, and "ornament-B.eps" for the star ornament. Copy the one you want to make on to the hard disk, and open it with Illustrator.

2

2. Tile with the pattern

Register the pattern you want to use in "Swatch" (see p181). Click on the "Select" tool and select the object on the document. Select the pattern you have saved to paint the object. Tile the object with the pattern.

3

3. Print

Set the paper and print the pattern.

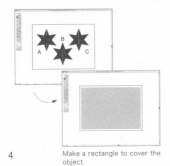

4

Make a rectangle to cover the object

4. Draw a rectangle and tile with the pattern

Now make the reverse side of each part of the ornament. Choose "Rectangle Tool". Create a rectangle that is big enough to cover the object you made in 2. (Make the rectangle one size bigger). When choosing the color, think about how it will go with the object colored in 2 and how it will look when finished. Print out the rectangle onto paper.

The object printed out in 3

cardboard

The object printed out in 4

5

Put the cardboard between the papers and glue together

6

Make a hole

5. Position the cardboard and glue

Place the cardboard between the pieces of paper made in 3 and 4, and glue them together.

6. Make a hole

Cut out the parts along the lines and make slits where indicated. Make a hole for threading.

[ornament-A]

①Push B into A and lock them in

②Push C into B and lock them in to assemble

7. Assemble and put thread through

Follow the diagram to assemble the parts together. At the end, cut the thread to the desired length and thread it through the hole.

Now your original paper ornaments are ready to hang!

Try different patterns and colors for more variety.

[ornament-B]

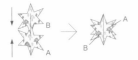

①Join A and B together using the slits

7

②Insert C as shown in the diagram

How to make a "tea-cozy"

A tea-cozy is essential in winter to keep your tea warm. With a hand made tea-cozy with a seasonal pattern, you will look forward to teatime!

1 [teacozy-outside.eps]
Note: The tea-cozy is designed to fit a tea pot approx. 18cm wide × 11cm deep × 13cm high

2

3

○You will need:

Canvas cloth specially made for printing (2 for outside), quilted fabric (for inside) ribbon (approx. width 2.5cm × length 10cm), sewing machine (if not available, hand stitch), sewing needle, marking pencil

1. Open the mount data

Find the "teacozy-outside.eps" file in the "Template" folder in the attached CD-ROM. Copy it on to the hard disk and open it with Illustrator.

2. Tile with the patterns

Register the pattern you want to use in "Swatch" (see p181). Click on the "Select" tool and select the object on the document. Select the pattern you have saved to paint. Before you choose the pattern, think about how it will look when finished, and how it will go with the fabric lining.

3. Print out the design on the canvas cloth

Set the cloth in the printer. Print two of the same designs as two pieces of fabric will be sewn together to make the outside part. Here, we're using canvas with a covering of PET film on the back. (NB: all cloth for printing has a printing side. Follow the instructions of your own printer for details of settings). Trim the excess all around and peel off the PET film on the back.

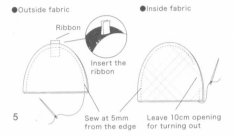

4 [teacozy-inside.eps]

Mark with marking pencil and cut quilt fabric

●Outside fabric

Ribbon

Insert the ribbon

●Inside fabric

5

Sew at 5mm from the edge

Leave 10cm opening for turning out

6

Inside fabric (the reverse side)

Outside fabric (the front side)

Sew at 5mm from the edge

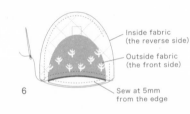

① Turn the right side out

②

Sew up the opening

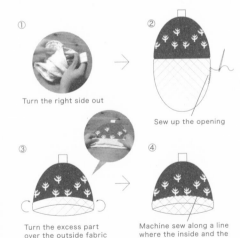

③

Turn the excess part over the outside fabric

④

Machine sew along a line where the inside and the outside fabrics meet

7

4. Cut fabric for the inside

Find the "teacozy-inside.eps" file in the "Template" folder in the attached CD-ROM. Copy it on to the hard disk and open it with Illustrator. Print it out on paper and cut into shape. Using this shape as a pattern, cut the quilted fabric to make two identical shapes.

The fabric lining is 5cm longer than the outside fabric. The excess fabric will be turned over later.

5. Sew

Place the two pieces of outside fabric right sides together. Insert the ribbon as shown in the diagram, and sew together at 5mm from the edge. Turn inside out the outside fabric. For the inside, place the two fabric right insides together and sew at 5mm from the edge, leaving an opening for turning out.

6. Sew together

Put the outside part into the inside pouch. Sew them together as shown in the diagram.

7. Turn the right side out and then turn the excess part up

① Turn the right side out. ② Check if the tea-cozy looks the same as in the diagram, then sew up the opening. ③ Push the inside part inwards and turn the excess part up as shown in the diagram. ④ Machine sew along the line where the inside and the outside fabrics meet to secure the overlap.

Now you have your original tea-cozy!

A matching pot-mat and coaster will make a lovely addition.

How to make a "puzzle calendar"

You can decorate your shelf with this cute and intriguing calendar, or fold it up and carry it with you. You can play with it like a puzzle by changing the way you fold it.

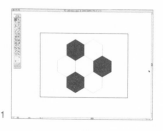

○You will need:

Drawing paper, printing paper, cutter, cutting mat, spray glue (if not available use liquid glue or glue stick), ruler, cutter, stylus (or you can use a ball-point pen that has no ink left or a pro-pelling pencil without the lead)

1. Open the mount data

Find the "calendar.eps" file in the "Template" folder in the attached CD-ROM. Copy it on to the hard disk, and open it with Illustrator.

2. Design with patterns

One hexagonal calendar has three months on one side, making a six month calendar using both sides. First, make the three month calendar.

Design days, months, and days of the week on hexagonal shapes that are not painted black. ("calendar2008.eps" in "Template" folder has calendar data so you can do this easily.)

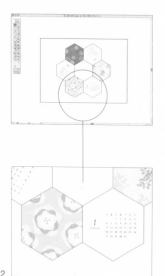

Next, to paint the black hexagonal shapes, choose the pattern for each month. Register the pattern in "Swatch" (see p181) and paint them. Make sure to arrange a month on the right side and a pattern for that month on the left.

3

Glue to drawing paper

3. Print out and glue on drawing paper

Print out the design onto paper. Spray glue the back of the printed paper and glue it onto drawing paper.

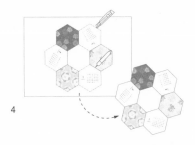

4

4. Make creases and cut

Follow the diagram to make creases on the lines between the patterns and the calendar. Cut out the shape along the outside lines. Now one side is complete.

5. Make the next three month calendar

Repeat 1-2 to make the next three month calendar. This time cut the printed paper first. Then glue it to the object made in 4. Make sure each pattern has another pattern at the other side that matches one month for another month.

5

Make sure that a patterned section is glued to a patterned section

6. Fold along the creases

Fold along the creases made in 4 as shown in the diagram.

Now your original calendar is ready to use!

Change the way the calendar is folded and you will get a different combination.

6

Mountain fold

Valley fold

Petit Pattern Book: Autumn & Winter
License Agreement of the Software

1. License

1) This License Agreement is a legal agreement between you (the "User"), who purchased the product Petit Pattern Book: Autumn & Winter, and BNN, Inc. ("BNN"), in respect of the attached CD-ROM entitled Petit Pattern Book: Autumn & Winter ("Software"). The User agrees to be bound by the terms of this License Agreement by installing, copying, or using the Software. BNN grants the User the right to use a copy of the Software on one personal computer for the exclusive use of the User.

2) The User may modify, edit, or combine the materials included in the Software except the cases specified in "2. Limitations" ; the User has the right to use the Software principally for design of the following objects.
- ○ Digital media including websites.
- ○ Use them as a graphic tool for creating shop interiors, signs, or for free wrapping services at the counter.
- ○ Leaflets, flyers, posters, direct mail, catalogues, pamphlets, and other tools for advertisement or sales promotion.
- ○ Goods, clothes, greeting cards, name cards and other articles for personal production and use. (The Software may be used for personal, professional, and commercial purposes, provided that the articles produced are not offered for sale. The User may not sell articles made with the Software, even when of a personal nature. Please read the following Limitations carefully.)

2. Limitations

The User is not licensed to do any of the following:
1) Copy the Software, unless copying it is unavoidable to enable it to be used on one personal computer.
2) License, or otherwise by any means permit, any other person to use the Software.
3) Use the Software to design of products for distribution(for printed matter on sale, e.g. books and magazines).
4) For wrapping merchandise or paid gift-wrapping services.
5) As a part of the brand image of a company (even when this is still under consideration for the future).
6) Use the Software for the commercial production of postcards, name cards, or any other articles, or sell any such articles made using the Software.
7) Provide downloading services using the Software (including greeting card services).
8) Create an environment which allows the original data to be downloaded when you show one of the Software patterns on a home page.
9) Use the Software in order to produce any software or other products for sale.
10) Acquire the copyright in any material in the Software or any object you have created using the Software.
11) Use the Software to create obscene, scandalous, abusive or slanderous works.

We will be more than happy to discuss your needs with you if you are interested in using our materials for commercial designs or product sales. Please contact us on the following number.
○ 2m09cmGRAPHICS, Inc. (fax : +81-3-3470-2356 e-mail : info@209g.com)

3. Copyright and other intellectual property

BNN or its suppliers reserves the copyright and other intellectual property rights in the Software. When specifying the User's copyright of a product made using the Software, please also write "©2007 2m09cmGRAPHICS, Inc." .

4. Exclusion of damages

In no event shall BNN be liable for any damages whatsoever (including but not limited to, damages for loss of profit or loss of data) related to the use or inability to use of the Software or use of materials in the Software.

5. Termination of this License Agreement

If the User breaches this License Agreement, BNN has the right to withdraw the User's License granted on the basis hereof.

おしゃれなパターン素材集
Petit Pattern Book

水玉・ストライプ
Dots & Stripes
ISBN：4-86100-384-9

花柄・リーフ
Flowers & Leaves
ISBN：978-4-86100-385-1

北欧・ファブリック
Scandinavian Style
ISBN：978-4-86100-386-8

和・きもの柄
Japanese Style
ISBN：978-4-86100-390-5

キッズ・トイ
Kids & Toys
ISBN：978-4-86100-506-0

チェック・ニット
Check & Knit
ISBN：978-4-86100-507-7

シンプル・ナチュラル
Simple & Natural
ISBN：978-4-86100-522-0

ポップ・モダン
Pop & Modern
ISBN：978-4-86100-523-7

春・夏
Spring & Summer
ISBN：978-4-86100-543-5

秋・冬
Autumn & Winter
ISBN：978-4-86100-542-8

おしゃれなパターン素材集
秋・冬

2007年10月25日　初版第1刷発行
2008年11月5日　初版第2刷発行

アートディレクション　中山正成（2m09cmGRAPHICS）

ブックデザイン　　　　内田槙子（2m09cmGRAPHICS）

写真撮影　　　　　　　前田幸恵

パターンデザイン　　　2m09cmGRAPHICS

編集　　　　　　　　　石井早耶香

翻訳　　　　　　　　　R.I.C.出版株式会社

発行人　　　　　　　　籔内康一

発行所　　　　　　　　株式会社ビー・エヌ・エヌ新社
　　　　　　　　　　　〒104-0042
　　　　　　　　　　　東京都中央区入船3-7-2　35山京ビル
　　　　　　　　　　　fax 03-5543-3108　e-mail info@bnn.co.jp

印刷・製本　　　　　　株式会社 シナノ